Adventures
of the
Iditarod Air Force

ADVENTURES
of the
IDITAROD AIR FORCE

True Stories about the Pilots
Who Fly for Alaska's
Famous Sled Dog Race

Ted Mattson

Illustrations by Sandy Jamieson

Epicenter Press
Fairbanks/Seattle

Epicenter Press Inc. is a regional press founded in Alaska whose interests include but are not limited to the arts, history, environment, and diverse cultures and lifestyles of the North Pacific and high latitudes. We seek both the traditional and innovative in publishing quality nonfiction tradebooks, contemporary art and photography giftbooks, and destination travel guides emphasizing Alaska, Washington, Oregon, and California.

The Iditarod Trail Committee® holds registered trademarks for the following terms and language: Iditarod®, Iditarod Trail Committee®, Iditarod Trail Alaska®, Alaska where men are men and women win the Iditarod®, The Last Great Race®, 1,049 miles®, Anchorage to Nome®, and Mushing the Iditarod Trail®.

Editor: Don Graydon
Cover design: Elizabeth Watson
Inside design: Don Graydon
Cover and text illustrations: Sandy Jamieson

Text © 1997 Ted Mattson
Illustrations © 1997 Sandy Jamieson

Library of Congress Catalog Card Number: 96-61936
ISBN 0-945397-59-3

To order single copies of *Adventures of the Iditarod Air Force,* send $14.95 (Washington residents add $1.23 state sales tax) plus $5 for priority mail shipping to: Epicenter Press, Box 82368, Kenmore, WA 98028.

Booksellers: Retail discounts are available from our trade distributor, Graphic Arts Center Publishing, Portland, Oregon; phone 800-452-3032.

PRINTED IN CANADA
First printing, January 1997
10 9 8 7 6 5 4 3 2 1

This book is for Larry Thompson
and for those who followed:

John Adams, Dennis Albert, David Alborn, Surge Amundsen, Daryl Anderson, Eep Anderson, Wayne Anderson, Jerry Austin, Mike Barbarick, Gary Baugh, Bill Bear, Tom Beard, Tim Betz, Russ Bevins, Mark Bills, Bruce Bishop, Peter Blackmon, Troy Blaylock, David Bogard, Burt Bomhoff, Don Bowers, Tom Bukowski, Brent Bunch, Richard Burmeister, Mike Carlton, Denver Carney, Wade Charles, Ken Chase, Ross Clement, Jim Cook, Danny Davidson, Dave Davis, Leonard Davis, Jimmy Demientieff, Drew Dix, Warren "Ace" Dodson, Dave Donaldson, Richard Dowling, Dick Eddlestein, Bob Elliot, Jim Ellis, Carl Emmons, Frank Everett, Dave Fetzner, Art Fields, Bill Firmin, Dick Forsgren, Keith Forsgren, Steve Foster, Jim Fredenhagen, Victoria Fredenhagen, Orv Gilbert, Wayne Gilmore, Boyd Gochenaour, Andy Greenblatt, Ed Gurtler, Roger Hackett, Sandy Hamilton, Bert Hanson, Glen Hanson, Todd Hardwick, Fred Herman, Irv Hobbs, Mike Horne, Richard Huff, Eric Johnson, John Johnson, Mike Jonrowe, Danny Jorgenson, Peter Kalamarides, Jim Kershner, Vern Kingsford, Jim Kintz, Howard Knutson, Wayne Koecher, George Konrad, Mike Koskovich, Bill Kramer, Anna Lampley, Jim Leach, Ty Lee, Al Lewis, Tommy Likos, Ron Linder, Kris Lundt, Dick Mackey, Bob Magnuson, Ted Mattson, Sam Maxwell, Bill Mayer, Chris McDonnell, Tom McGillivary, David Mersereau, Mike Minsch, Von Mitten, Kenn Moon, Carol Moore, Mike Moore, Mike Morales, Philip Morgan, Bruce Moroney, George Murphy, Roger Nordlum, John Norris, Denny O'Neal, Tony Oney Sr., Tony Oney Jr., Bruce Palmer, Wally Parks, Rodger Patch, Greg Peppard, Franklin Peterson, Pete Peterson, Joe Phillips, Michael Pietre, Tom Prunty, Richard Pulley, Mike Radford, Joe Redington Sr., John Reed, Barry Rempel, Les Reynolds, Ronnie Rosander, Reagan Russey, Dale Schramm, Lynn Shawback, Roger Sires, Timothy Skala, Jim Smarz, Kathy (Mackey) Smith, Hugo Snell, Joe Soha, Tony Spoonemore, Don Stone, Floyd Tetpon, Steve Theno, Scott Thorson, Gene Tizel, Tony Turinsky, Bill Turner, Pat Varney, David Vidmar, Dennis Weston, Steve Widmer, Steve Wooliver, Mike Yerkes, and Kevin Zilco. Also, Alaska Airlines, Alaska Air Guides, Bering Air, Big Country Flying, Galena Air, Harold's Air, Hermen's Air, Mark Air, Munz Northern Airlines, Northern Air Cargo, Peninsula Airways, Ryan Air, Susitna Air, Wien Air Alaska, and Wilbur's Air.

This honor roll of Iditarod Air Force volunteers comes from incomplete records and fading memories. Please let me know if you have a name to add.

Contents

Preface

I first envisioned this book as a history of the volunteer flying corps known informally throughout Alaska as the Iditarod Air Force. It ended up instead to be a series of aviation-related tales of adventure along the now-famous route of the Iditarod Trail Sled Dog Race—glimpses of what goes on behind the scenes of this unique sporting event. But oddly enough, what emerged was still the history of this exceptional group of pilot volunteers.

A word of caution: while pilots may brag about their exploits, they also sometimes drastically understate those same feats. At times they will do both simultaneously. As you read these anecdotes, you may find yourself asking, "What is fact and what is fancy?"

I had the good fortune to be part of this remarkable group of flyers for four years, piloting my own Super Cub along the Iditarod Trail. What you are about to read is their story, not mine, although it was impossible not to get mixed up in it at times. Hopefully, my thirty-one years of flying experience enabled me to filter out the tall tales from the true.

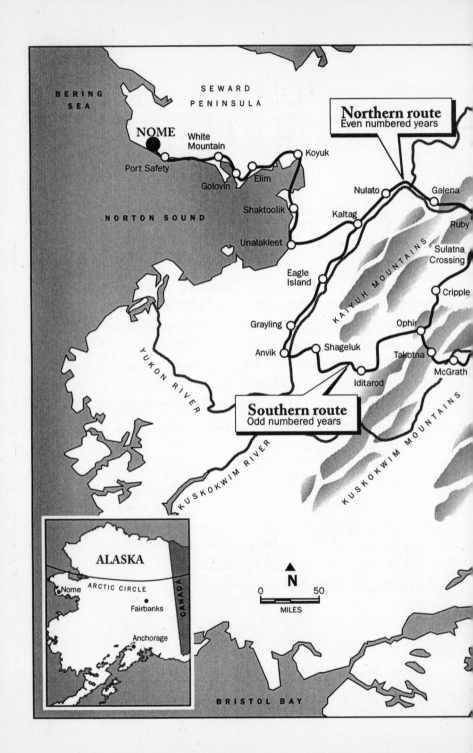

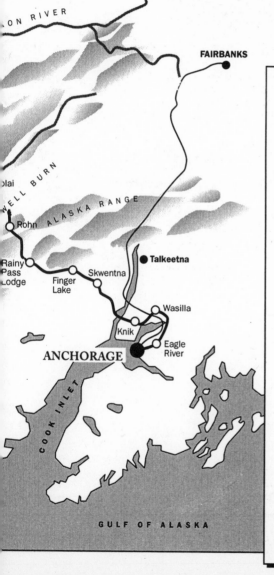

IDITAROD TRAIL SLED DOG RACE

CHECKPOINTS	MILEAGE
Anchorage to Eagle River	20
Eagle River to Wasilla	29
Wasilla to Knik	14
Knik to Skwentna	88
Skwentna to Finger Lake	45
Finger Lake to Rainy Pass Lodge	30
Rainy Pass Lodge to Rohn	40
Rohn to Nikolai	93
Nikolai to McGrath	48
McGrath to Takotna	23
Takotna to Ophir	38
SOUTHERN ROUTE	
Ophir to Iditarod	90
Iditarod to Shageluk	65
Shageluk to Anvik	25
Anvik to Grayling	18
Grayling to Eagle Island	70
Eagle Island to Kaltag	70
NORTHERN ROUTE	
Ophir to Cripple	60
Cripple to Ruby	112
Ruby to Galena	52
Galena to Nulato	52
Nulato to Kaltag	42
Kaltag to Unalakleet	90
Unalakleet to Shaktoolik	38
Shaktoolik to Koyuk	58
Koyuk to Elim	48
Elim to Golovin	28
Golovin to White Mountain	18
White Mountain to Port Safety	55
Port Safety to **Nome**	22

Acknowledgments

This book could never have been created without the generous cooperation of the Iditarod pilots. Special thanks, though, must go to Don Bowers for the use of his Iditarod journals and his other notes and papers. Don had been planning to write his own version of the Iditarod Air Force story, but instead came down with "dog mushingitis." I'm also indebted to the other pilots and mushers who let me come to their homes with tape recorder and lists of questions or who took the time to talk with me on the phone.

Special appreciation goes to Joanne Potts and Jack Niggemyer at Iditarod race headquarters for their generous help, whether it was digging out material from the archives and from personal notes or answering my many questions or giving me advice on other sources of information.

Thanks also go out to those friends who offered feedback after reading part or all of the manuscript or listening to excerpts. Some folks stuck with me through four rewrites–a mark of real friendship.

And finally, to Don Graydon and the editors at Epicenter Press, who waded through the quagmire of a rough manuscript, my grateful thanks.

Introduction

Every March, a sled dog race is run from Anchorage up to Nome—and there are at least a couple schools of thought about its origin. If you are one of the volunteer pilots who fly above the trail each year, you tend to support the theory that the race is put on for your benefit so that you have an opportunity to sharpen your winter flying skills—bush flying at its best! The rest of the world, however, tends to support the view that the race is a commemorative of the diphtheria serum run of 1925, and that it gives mushers a chance to test themselves and their dogs against the elements in a land known for testing the hardiest of the hardy.

The fact is, neither view is totally correct. First of all, Joe Redington Sr. and Dick Mackey cut brush from much of the trail near Skwentna years before anyone associated the serum run to Nome with the present-day race trail. The race actually follows much of the route that was once the main artery from the seacoast near Seward into the gold fields at Iditarod. It just seems to make livelier history to say that the present-day Iditarod Trail follows the old sled dog trail that was used to get the lifesaving serum to the isolated, diphtheria-threatened village of Nome. But the race really follows a combination of both of those historic trails.

Even in 1925, an airplane could have taken the serum to Nome, had the weather cooperated. But it was 56 below zero, a bit risky for both airplane and pilot, and the only qualified flyer was out of the state at the time. So the decision was made to load the serum onto a train bound for Nenana up near Fairbanks, where courageous sled dogs and mushers began the relay that covered the remaining 674 roadless miles through unforgiving wilderness in record time to save the village of Nome—and thus become immortalized in Alaska history.

The airplane, which ultimately replaced the sled dog team and made Alaska the place it is today, got left out of the history books on that one.

One thing is certain: the annual Iditarod Trail Sled Dog Race is a supreme test for dogs and mushers—and for the pilots and airplanes that fly in support. In 1973, through the efforts of dog-mushing enthusiasts led by Joe Redington Sr.—Father of the Iditarod—the first race from Anchorage to Nome took place. Winner Dick Wilmarth made it to the finish line in just over 20 days. From a humble beginning, when no one was even sure a dog team could go that far, the race has captured the imaginations of adventurers the world over. The event now known as The Last Great Race was born.

Today, even ten days is too long to spend on the trail if you want the biggest share of a purse that has grown to some $400,000. Competing in the race represents a huge commitment. The fee for each team to enter was set for a long time at $1,049 (a dollar a mile); it's now $1,750. To be competitive, each musher might invest another $20,000 or more in equipment, supplies, training, and transportation. Whole lives revolve around the care and feeding and training of dogs just for the race—not unlike being on a dairy farm where life is governed by the morning and evening milkings.

The competitors who head up the trail each March carry with them a determination that the rest of us, who have not been bitten by the dog-mushing bug, can only wonder about. But a word of caution: no one is immune. A few of the volunteer pilots, letting curiosity get the best of them, have stepped onto the back runners of a sled just to see how it feels. Jerry Austin, who started flying the trail as a pilot volunteer, never got off. He has completed nineteen Iditarod races behind a team of dogs.

About seventy or eighty mushers sign up each year. Some never make it out of the chute; others fall out along the way for a multitude of reasons that couldn't be predicted beforehand. It's an understatement to say that it takes extraordinary ability plus strength, stamina, and luck to make it to the burled arch that marks the finish line in Nome. Any musher will assure you it takes all that and more.

Nobody makes it up the trail alone. Much credit is always given to the nearly two thousand volunteers needed to stage what has become one of the most grueling and inspirational sporting events of all time. At both ends of the route and at some two dozen checkpoints along the thousand-plus miles, volunteers help with communications, transportation, emergencies, and the logistics of everything from delivering dog food to keeping track of the race teams. You'll see checkers, race officials, radio operators, veterinarians, and pilots. They are the unsung heroes of the Iditarod, and the race would not take place without them.

The volunteers rally around the Iditarod just as they rally around Alaska itself, perfectly willing to accept arctic conditions, lack of roads, limited communications, or whatever. Among their rewards are mountains, glaciers, wild seacoasts, and lonely vistas so beautiful that you may forget to exhale. These volunteers are not prone to sit back in armchairs inside cozy living rooms and simply watch this land. They want to be out in it and experience the action, and they are among the race's biggest fans. The pilots are no exception.

Pilots loom in the background of every phase of the race. It is the airplane that has made the Iditarod the world event it has become. Without the airplane to deliver food and supplies and people to points along the route, the race would be more of a "sled freighting event" or a "camping trip." Without the airplane to transport camera crews, race fans would never have the thrill of seeing the mushers and their dogs in action.

Armchair race enthusiasts in the Lower 48 still find it hard to comprehend a wilderness so vast that a trail can bisect a thousand-mile chunk of it without crossing a road. Right from Dick Wilmarth's win that first year, the airplane played an integral role in the Iditarod. Over the years, as more and more pilots volunteered to lend a hand, the "Iditarod Air Force" came into being.

These pilots throw more than just themselves into each race. They also bring their airplanes, an investment rivaling even that of the most advanced of the racing kennels that vie for the big prize money. As a group, the pilots bring something like two million dollars worth of equipment into an event they have little control over. No pilot sits on the Iditarod Trail Committee's board of directors. As volunteers, the pilots may appear somewhat aloof–prima donnas by some standards. But when you realize they provided their services for much of the race's history without benefit of any reimbursement for damaged airplanes, it's easy to understand. Even though fuel and other incidentals have been provided since the beginning, anyone who flies knows that is only part of the cost of keeping a plane in the air. Insurance is now provided, but the tally left along the trail over the years is something too few hear about.

Not everyone who flies the trail is a volunteer, of course. Many bush air-taxi operators are involved, with some work done for hire and some provided just to help out. Major airlines and cargo carriers assist with special fares, rearranged schedules, and free dog-hauling services. Some pilots go to work for the media, which hire their own transportation out on the trail.

Often fun-loving and full of mischief, many of the Iditarod aviators–along with the mushers below–are hanging on to an era in Alaska that has all but passed into history. These pilots recall a time when flying was still very much seat-of-the-pants stuff. With all the pilots involved in the Iditarod, the result is a lot of flying activity associated with a few dozen mushers on the ground. And as might be expected, there are a lot of stories to tell.

1 Cream Puff

No matter how much everyone in Alaska wants the race to succeed, there are those who thoroughly regret they ever heard the word Iditarod. Just ask the pilot of *Cream Puff*.

Cream Puff, all decked out with a new yellow-on-white paint scheme over new fabric, came fluttering into the little checkpoint village of Skwentna on one of those blue-sky, sun-drenched days when the wind had forgotten to blow. The race was well under way, with most of the leading mushers already mounting the Alaska Range nearly a hundred miles distant. This was back when the Iditarod was still very much in its infancy.

Cream Puff's pilot, known in memory only as Rick, was energetic and eager to help. "I'm heading back to Anchorage empty," Rick told another volunteer. "Is there anything you'd want me to carry along?"

"Well," came the fateful reply, "we've got some dogs that have to go that way. Just go ask Larry."

LARRY THOMPSON—known as Mr. Iditarod Air Force for his years of work on the race—confesses that originally he "sort of got suckered" into working on the race when reporter-photographer Gordon Fowler of the *Anchorage Times* asked Larry to drop him off along the trail to take some photos. The Iditarod was desperate for media coverage in the early years. "You couldn't even buy press time in the beginning," Larry says.

One thing led to another, and suddenly Larry found himself helping here, there, and everywhere during the race, even though Gordon Fowler ended up not even covering it. But Gordon had arranged for the Iditarod Trail Committee to pay for Larry's fuel in exchange for Larry hauling veterinarian Jack Morris in his plane. Larry agreed, and the gun went off to start the race.

All of a sudden it was snowing, and Yentna Station reported it had not received some of its supplies. Could Larry drop some things off there? Then Skwentna needed supplies, and pretty soon Rainy Pass Lodge was calling in for some items. Larry and Doc Morris were hauling whatever needed hauling. Other pilots along the way helped wherever they could. Commercial carriers pitched in as well, hauling some loads for free. It seemed that everyone was giving their all to the Iditarod.

THE PILOT OF *CREAM PUFF* was clearly no exception on that rare sun-drenched day in Skwentna. Rick sought out Larry, who was busy loading his Cessna 180 with gear to be moved up the trail.

Larry was happy to show Rick how he could help, by ferrying a load of dogs back to Anchorage. Mushers were allowed to begin the race with a certain number of dogs, but often had to drop off animals who developed problems or became ill. The musher would haul an affected dog to the next checkpoint in the basket of the sled and drop it off to be inspected by a vet and then flown home.

"Do they bite?" Rick asked somewhat hesitantly.

"Never had one try it yet," Larry assured him.

"How many can I take?" Rick asked.

"Just open the door," Larry told him, "and start stuffing until you can't get anymore in."

This approach suited Larry's demanding work ethic, as summed up by another Iditarod pilot, Kathy (Mackey) Smith: "He never considered any airplane that could get off before the end of the runway to be fully loaded."

Larry tried to reassure Rick: "Don't worry. They'll settle right down once they're airborne. Someone will be at the other end to give you a hand when you arrive."

And so the dog-laden little Maule airplane wallowed into the air, doing its part to lend a hand in the big race. Unfortunately, the promised helper was nowhere to be seen as Rick landed on skis on Anchorage's frozen Lake Hood.

He carefully locked *Cream Puff's* doors and headed for race headquarters, searching for the dog handler. By the time Rick found the handler and they returned to the plane, the dogs had taken the matter of being locked up as a personal challenge and were now scattered everywhere on the ice. Some were lifting their legs to relieve themselves against the ski struts. Others were just sniffing around, enjoying their newfound freedom.

More startling yet was the sight of *Cream Puff*. Even for the dog handler–who was not a pilot, and who had not spent the last six months painstakingly refurbishing every inch of his favorite airplane–it was a scene that would be burned into memory. Every dog must have chewed its own way out through the fabric doors and sides of the little plane. In less than an hour, *Cream Puff* had been reduced to something resembling a hunk of Swiss cheese with wings.

2 Sea Ice

One thing the guys who fly the Iditarod Trail soon learn is that once the race reaches the seacoast, a whole new set of rules governs whether a pilot comes through unscathed. And being lucky doesn't hurt a bit. The vastness of the land and the severe weather are the most obvious worries, but a darker element also awaits, always changing and always dangerous: the unpredictable sea ice.

People who live along the east and west coasts of the United States, regardless of how far north they may be, don't normally associate winter with the ocean freezing over. The weather turns frigid, snow falls, the wind blows, winter storms crash on shore, and sea spray turns everyday objects into magnificent sculptures of ice. All of this happens in the Arctic, too, except that it all happens long before the heavy hand of winter finally presses down to squeeze the waters silent, covering them in a mantle of ice.

But beneath the ice, the sea does not give up easily. Below the frozen surface, the tides never rest. Offshore storms still make waves. The coasts are still buffeted by winds, but the water that would normally come crashing ashore is now forced to act in slow motion. The white ice-shrouded coasts move. Cracks open up, then come together again. Pressure ridges form. Huge chunks of glistening ice pile up and spill over each other, grinding their forms together, emitting rumbles that send shudders down the spine of anyone caught out on the ice when it's in the mood to move. The ice-covered ocean, frozen to the curve of the earth, can become open water in a matter of hours if the wind decides to float the ice pack out to sea. Always dangerous, sea ice can change as quickly as a politician's promise.

As THE IDITAROD MUSHERS come off the ice and onto Nome's Front Street for the final dash to the finish line, they have had ample opportunity to experience the arctic coast and the ice in all its moods, for it has been with them off and on for more than 250 miles, ever since Unalakleet. This final barrier of the race, the frozen seacoast, hits everyone squarely in the face, including the pilots of the Iditarod Air Force. No one who ventures into this land escapes winter's wrath. Pilot Danny Davidson found this out one nerve-racking day in Nome, as we'll soon see.

It's hard to explain Nome to someone who has never been there. The town is a singular place that can take hold of you and compel you to return. Set in a treeless, barren landscape, Nome greets visitors with a ramshackle array of buildings in all states of development and decomposition, their furnace exhaust plumes signaling the cold that hugs the land during race time. Nome takes the Last Great Race in its stride just as it has absorbed nearly a century's worth of history since three Swedes first found the rich placer deposit that turned the settlement into a raw frontier gold-mining town.

On this particular morning, Danny Davidson was asleep in his room along Front Street. He had managed to score one of the few rooms overlooking the Nome waterfront. His airplane was conveniently close by, securely tied down to ice screws set into the smooth sea ice fronting the town. An extension cord from the airplane's engine heater was plugged into an electrical outlet in his room.

Danny has flown for the Iditarod as much as anyone. Fourteen races at last count. His tall thin frame, dark curly hair, and mustachioed smile are readily recognized along the trail. If there's a party going on, or a joke being played on someone, Danny is sure to be in the middle of it.

He was suddenly jarred awake on this morning by the commotion of his fellow pilots.

"Danny! Danny! Wake up. Your airplane is drifting out to sea!"

ACCUSTOMED TO THE PRANKS of Iditarod pilots, Danny reacted calmly upon being awakened so early after a long and lively night along saloon-lined Front Street.

"Oh sure," he said, rolling his eyes. "And what do you suppose this cord is plugged into?" he asked, as he started pulling on the extension cord that ran out to his classy red

Cessna 180. Feeling no resistance on the cord, he jumped from bed and ran to the window. At first he had a hard time believing the sight that greeted his sleep-filled eyes. Floating on a huge sheet of sea ice, hundreds of yards offshore, was his securely tied-down Cessna. During the night, an offshore wind had sprung up. The tide came in as well, lifting the shore ice from its grounding. The wind had now backed down to a gentle breeze, but it was still slowly escorting the ice pack out into the Bering Sea, where the next scheduled stop was Russia. Danny watched as a crack cut through the mass of ice bearing his plane. The sea ice was breaking up as it moved away from shore.

Eric Pentilla of Evergreen Helicopters was quick to respond. He flew Danny and several others out onto the drifting ice, where they were soon standing beside the little plane. Everything that wasn't necessary for flight was taken to shore aboard the helicopter while a portable engine heater slowly brought life back into Danny's bird. The rescuers untied the ropes and salvaged the ice screws that held the plane in place. After last-minute checks, Danny started the engine.

The ice in front of the Cessna was dwindling as more and more pieces broke off and floated free. But a bit of luck was with Danny: slowly, almost imperceptibly, the ice "runway" was turning so that the plane faced into the breeze, just right for a takeoff attempt. Danny waited, knowing he needed every advantage. But a gnawing fear wouldn't go away. If the ice cracked again across what was left of the strip in front of him, he would be running for the helicopter, and his airplane would be doomed.

Pushing the throttle forward and locking it, Danny felt the Cessna move ahead. He dropped his hand down to the flap lever and waited for the airspeed to build. The dryness in his mouth increased; there was nothing to swallow. His palms were sweating inside the fleece-lined gloves, and cool trickles ran down from his armpits. The plane raced toward the end of the ice runway. Danny wondered how the seawater might feel.

He glanced at the dials. The airspeed was climbing, but it wasn't there yet. Again his throat muscles tightened as his hand automatically eased at the flaps. He knew he was in "ground effect"—that illusion of more lift than the airplane really had—so he kept the nose down, not daring to go for the altitude that every fiber in his body cried out for. This was no time to get sloppy.

Black and threatening, frigid water was sliding just beneath the skis. The 180 was holding its own. But was it gaining speed or just moving along in ground effect? It was hard to tell with no outside references. A lifetime passed. Then another. When he dared take his eyes off the horizon, the airspeed indicator was well into the green. His shoulders relaxed as he eased back on the yoke and reduced the flaps. Danny was smiling as he banked the plane toward Nome.

Front Street saw lots of Iditarod Air Force celebrating that night, and you can be sure it was not for the dogs that crossed the finish line.

3 An Ophir Incident

If awards were ever given under the burled arch in Nome for favorite checkpoints along the Iditarod Trail, Ophir would definitely be a front-runner. Ophir is a gold-mining ghost town about 475 trail miles from the Anchorage starting line and in the heart of the still-active Innoko gold-mining district. But it is not gold that attracts people to Ophir during the race. It is Dick and Audra Forsgren and the hospitality of their cabin along the spruce- and birch-lined banks of the Innoko River where it winds through broad valleys on its way to the Yukon.

Dick and Audra have owned the historic cabin since the 1960s and have hosted the checkpoint for all but the first race. Dick, still energetic and feisty in retirement, has handled several Iditarod positions, including flying for the volunteer air force. Son Keith grew up to eventually fly the trail as well, and now is a pilot for United Parcel Service. Audra's extensive collection of photos and memorabilia from all those years will someday be as historic as the cabin itself. The cabin, solidly built by a Swede for his mail-order bride in the 1930s, is a haven for all who pass. If you're lucky enough to be there for the annual turkey dinner during race time, you might think you had been transported back in time. No modern electronic oven has ever replaced the Forsgrens' old-fashioned wood cookstove for producing mouth-watering vittles.

Despite a substantial landing strip nearby, most pilots coming into Ophir opt for the daring landing on the horseshoe bend of the little Innoko River. These pilots seem to thrive on the challenge of the squirrelly winds, the water that overflows on top of the ice, and the deep snows.

To make matters even more interesting, the overflow is usually hidden beneath the snow. In the Alaskan Interior in winter, it's possible to land a ski plane and to then step out into snow that is chest deep—with water coming up to your knees.

Every year the new air force volunteers are warned about the hazards of working off the Innoko River, but most have to try the horseshoe landing on for size. Audra's scrapbook has enough photos of bent airplanes to prove the point. There was the time, for instance, that Bert Hanson nearly destroyed his brother's Cessna 185 during the 1988 race.

THE STORY BEGINS WITH Stuart Nelson, the veterinarian on duty at Ophir, who had sent word back to the checkpoint at McGrath that he was getting low on dog-foot ointment. He had also sent some advice to any pilot who might make the delivery: instead of attempting the tricky river landing, "just throw the stuff out the window on your way past with a ribbon attached."

Bert Hanson was en route to the Yukon—piloting his brother Glen's plane, with veterinarian Wayne McGee aboard—when Stuart's request for ointment came over the radio. Wayne told Bert he had an extra supply of the ointment stashed in his gear.

Bert decided to land on the Innoko. What could the vet at Ophir possibly know about landing an airplane on the river?

Stuart was kneeling down, examining a dog, when he heard the plane overhead. He looked up and saw it circle, setting up the approach for a landing on the horseshoe bend.

"It couldn't be the ointment," he thought. "Must be someone else." He continued working. Moments later he heard a dull thud. He walked to where he could see down over the riverbank. There were Bert and Wayne, crawling out the doors of the upside-down airplane, which was partially buried in snow.

Another airplane soon landed, then another. Stuart marveled at how fast word seems to travel in the bush. Everyone pitched in, and Bert's brother's airplane was soon right-side up once more, although it would take a good deal of work before it could fly again.

Veterinarian McGee gave the dog-foot ointment to veterinarian Nelson, who then started back to the cabin, driving Dick Forsgren's snowmachine. Dick volunteered to fly Wayne McGee to where he had been heading when he ended up in the plane crash. Dick asked someone nearby to clear him for takeoff when he started his Super Cub.

In the deep snow, Dick had trouble powering out onto the takeoff track. Then his wing caught some bank-side alders, further holding him from turning toward the track. Dick obviously did not see the innocent snowmachine that his Cub was about to devour.

Pilot Don Bowers gives the best description of what happened next. In his journal, Bowers wrote:

"The vet took one look at the Super Cub charging down on him at full power and jumped headfirst into the snow. Dick's Cub then chewed up the top of the snowmachine just like in the movies—pieces of plastic, metal, and seat cushion flying everywhere. When the engine finally stopped, the Cub was mounted firmly atop the partially digested snowmachine."

Dick threw open the door of his Cub and turned to the fellow who had cleared him to start the engine.

"Clear, hell!" he thundered.

The final tally: two bent airplanes; one mashed snowmachine; a couple of bruised pilot egos; no serious injuries. Wayne McGee could claim the distinction of being in two airplane crashes in one day.

The postscript to this incident is that the airplanes were flown out again. Dick Forsgren was on his way in his Super Cub as soon as he straightened the propeller. Bert Hanson, a captain for Reeve Aleutian Airlines and a licensed aircraft mechanic, hooked the wing on his brother's plane to the winch of a miner's bulldozer and bent it back down into place, then sandwiched the wing between pieces of steel. With the landing gear replaced, Bert flew the plane out.

It should be noted that aircraft insurance was unheard of along the Iditarod Trail until recently. Incidents like these were considered "gifts" to the Iditarod cause.

4 The Farewell Burn Burn

News came up the trail to Nikolai that one of the trail breakers had had an accident with his snow-machine, somewhere between Rohn and Nikolai, and had suffered a heart attack. The accident occurred right in the middle of what is widely regarded as the most dreaded part of the trail, the Farewell Burn. At Iditarod headquarters in McGrath, race manager Jack Niggemyer grabbed chief pilot Danny Davidson, and they flew immediately to Nikolai.

Details of the accident were sketchy, but one trail breaker was sure there was no place at the accident scene to land a fixed-wing plane. This, after all, was the Farewell Burn—a tangle of burned-over trees, often without snow cover, a tough territory for mushers, dogs, or airplanes.

The Farewell Burn was first called the Bear Creek Burn when it began in the summer of 1977. Spawned by lightning strikes, it became one of Alaska's most devastating forest fires, burning 312,000 acres. The fire swept through an area

35

that heats to broiling temperatures in summer, even without lightning, an area where clouds of mosquitoes challenge the sanity of a summer visitor. In winter, river ice can be 5 feet thick in this land where wolves and moose square off regularly.

The area eventually became known as the Farewell Burn because of its proximity to the Farewell area, which lies across the race route northwest of Rohn. It is one of the most talked about, least reliable sections of the trail because of all the fire damage. The scars of wilderness fires can linger through several lifetimes, and mushers will be struggling with the Farewell Burn for many races to come. There are places within the Burn to land an airplane safely, but it's more likely you'd be eating what's left of charred spruce with a forced landing.

Jack Niggemyer called for help from the National Guard in Fairbanks, which agreed to dispatch a helicopter rescue unit. The helicopter would stop in Nikolai to pick up the trail breaker who had brought word of the accident, and he would lead rescuers to the site.

The race was in full swing and both Danny and Jack had their hands full with race business, but they decided to sit tight in Nikolai, waiting for word from the rescue crew over the two-way radio. Hours dragged by. Finally, in desperation, they decided to fly back to McGrath, where they would also have access to a telephone.

As they flew out of Nikolai, a column of black smoke in the Farewell Burn caught their attention. Danny got on the radio, but couldn't raise anyone. Eyeing the fuel gauges, he saw he didn't have enough gas to fly to the smoky area and back to McGrath. But both men sensed something terrible had happened: the helicopter must have crashed, and they would be first on the scene. This explained why they hadn't received any word from the rescue team. Danny turned his plane toward the smoke. "If they need help, I'll just have to find a place to get us down," he told Jack. "We'll worry about the gas later."

WHAT THEY FOUND was not a wreck, but a party. From the air, the men could see a group of trail breakers casually sitting in the snow around a huge bonfire, drinking coffee. Slowly the story came together over the small hand-held radio that the trail breakers carried. The radio had not been strong enough to transmit to Danny when he first called.

The trail breakers reported that the helicopter had already come and gone, taking the injured man away. When the trail breakers first heard the chopper, they fired a flare. It failed, landing in a nearby pile of brush and debris. They fired a second flare, which brought the helicopter in for a landing. Medics on the chopper determined that the trail breaker had only cracked a rib when his machine rolled over on him; no serious injuries, no heart attack. So they whisked him off to McGrath for some rest, instead of to a Fairbanks hospital. The "emergency" was over.

But meanwhile, the dud flare was still smoldering. Fanned by the blades of the helicopter, the flare set fire to the brush. The trail breakers, relieved that their companion was out of danger, decided to enjoy the warmth of the fire.

The blaze had grown past the billowing black-smoke stage that first attracted Danny and Jack, and it now looked like a big old-fashioned bonfire: the Farewell Burn Burn, as the trail breakers called it.

As the last of the story was pieced together, Danny was already turning the plane toward McGrath, its fuel gauges on empty. He headed for the relative safety of the frozen Kuskokwim River, grabbing all the altitude he could. About 5 miles from home, the engine sucked the last of the gas fumes, and Danny dead-sticked a landing on the river, talking to McGrath radio the whole time.

It wasn't long before another Iditarod Air Force plane arrived with cans of gas. By the time they got back to race headquarters in McGrath, the "victim" was finishing his second cheeseburger at Rosa's.

And why hadn't the rescue crew or the victim radioed a report to Jack and Danny?

"No sense calling when there wasn't much wrong," the fellow reasoned to Jack.

A few days later, the United States government sent Iditarod headquarters a bill for the rescue. Jack studied the bill. To look at Jack, you might see a cross between a Haight-Ashbury flower child and a grizzled Yukon prospector—not exactly the person you'd expect to be responsible for a multimedia megabucks sporting event like the Last Great Race. But Jack has been able to carry it off while retaining a sense of humor and a humble matter-of-factness about the whole thing. Looking at the bill, he simply shook his head in mock disbelief and smiled as he remarked, "The bill was only for $8,000."

5 Hanging by a Thread

While mushers on the trail fight it out for a $50,000 first prize, the pilots of the Iditarod Air Force are up in the air, sometimes risking everything– and with no chance at a prize. Aluminum doesn't come cheap when it's fabricated into anything that has to do with aircraft. Bend that piece of aluminum, and all of a sudden your experience level, and your costs, soar. It's the kind of experience that most pilots spend their careers trying to avoid.

When the race is over, and the mushers and dogs and most of the volunteers are safely back home, pilots who have brought their "piece of aluminum" along to support the race are likely as not still stuck somewhere, waiting for the weather to improve or helping clean out one of the remote checkpoints along the trail.

When you eventually cross the Alaska Range for that last time on your final leg to Anchorage, there is always a sense of relief: "I've made it again!" Another race is behind you, and there will be lots of "hangar flying" in the months ahead as you retell the tales of the race. Somehow, this last leg of the trail seems civilized, almost tame. It's easy to let your guard down.

These may not have been the exact thoughts going through Dave Alborn's mind at the end of the 1990 race as he piloted his Cessna 180 through the mountains at nearly 7,000 feet. On his regular job, Dave was a captain with Mark Air, a professional in every sense of the word. The 180, loaded with people and gear, purred smoothly along in the evening air. Mount Susitna was up ahead, and the first lights of Anchorage dotted the horizon. They were almost home, but everyone seems to get a lesson in humility when they least want it, because that's when the engine decided to quit.

There was no panic in Dave's voice as he contacted the Anchorage flight center, giving his position and situation. Miraculously, Dave found an open spot and brought the plane down unscathed except for a dinged wingtip. No one was hurt. It was too late to get a helicopter up and running before dark. Dave and his passengers would have to wait until morning. The airplane was tied down, and they all spent the night around a roaring fire. Dave was happy. He still had his life, and he still had his airplane—an especially important point back in the days when insurance wasn't part of the Iditarod flying package.

MORNING FINALLY CAME, as did the rescue helicopter. Passengers and gear were lifted out. Meanwhile, the 180 was readied for its own ride back to civilization; this fixed-wing beauty would be ingloriously slung beneath a helicopter. Spoilers were attached to the wing's upper surface to prevent the plane from trying to fly up into the chopper. The plane was attached to a triangle hookup at the end of a 50-foot cable from the helicopter. One portion of the triangle went back to the tail to keep the plane straight and level in the air. The other two parts were attached at the wing roots to take the weight of the plane. And they were off.

All seemed to be going well. Dave's wife, Mary, was waiting near Lake Hood in Anchorage with a video camera when the helicopter arrived with the family's pride and joy precariously dangling from what appeared, to Mary, like a mere thread. "The 180 looked pretty forlorn hanging there," she recalls.

Mary was not prepared for what she was about to witness through the camera's viewfinder. Evidently one of the plane's spoilers had come loose as helicopter and plane neared the airport. The wind decided to turn squirrelly right then, and the helicopter pilot was quickly in danger of losing control. A bit of bush-rescue protocol suddenly became very relevant: the one thing you automatically agree to when you sling-load an airplane out of the bush is that the helicopter pilot is not responsible for any damage that might occur.

The scene that unfurled before Mary's camera seemed as orchestrated as an MGM action shoot. The helicopter pilot punched the red button, letting Dave Alborn's beautiful, newly painted 180 fall earthward. On the way down, it hit the top edge of a two-story building, then toppled onto two pickup trucks parked on the street below.

Mary managed to keep the camera focused during all the action, and she can laugh when she tells the story now. Little did anyone know at the time that the 180 was not the only airplane the Alborns would "contribute" to the success of the Iditarod. Three years later, a freak accident cost Dave a Cessna 185. The Alborns ended up investing quite a bundle in a dog race they can never hope to win.

6 Miracle at Golovin

The year that Martin Buser was pushing toward his first Iditarod win, Chris McDonnell and I were flying our Super Cubs, hauling photographers Jeff Schultz and Jim Brown wherever they wanted to go along the trail. The morning was bright and clear as we arrived in Koyuk, although a bit of ground blizzard was blowing out on Norton Sound. Just about every reporter covering the 1992 race was in Koyuk as the competition neared an end, and a carnival-like atmosphere pervaded the town. The trailing mushers were just starting out onto the ice of Norton Sound while Buser tried to take a nap despite a TV camera thrust almost into his face. The unpredictable arctic weather was soon to turn this carnival into near-tragedy for two men.

Chris and Jeff planned to fly on toward White Mountain so they would be in place when the race leaders arrived. Everything was building up to a last-minute dash to the finish line in Nome. Meanwhile, Jim and I flew back toward Shaktoolik to deliver some frozen meat. We were kept from making the delivery earlier by a ground blizzard, in which the wind picks up loose, dry arctic snow and sweeps it along. The blizzards may extend only several feet above the ground, with the sun and blue sky glistening overhead. Some ground blizzards, however, reach high into the sky, creating a featureless landscape impossible to navigate without instruments.

As we flew across the ice toward Shaktoolik, we spotted Susan Butcher, head down against the blowing snow, her dogs picking their way along the trail. Jim wanted to set down for a photo. I turned and headed back into the wind, looking for a smooth landing spot.

Below us, we could see the endless line of spruce limbs that had been inserted into holes chopped in the ice, to serve as guideposts for the mushers along this part of the trail. The branches looked strangely out of place—the only in-line forest I've ever seen. All I could do was line up on the row of "trees" and let the Cub find its way down through the blowing snow and onto the sea ice a mile or so in front of one of the most competitive mushers in the race.

Susan's head was still down in an attempt to get some protection from the wind when her team finally reached us. The dogs, sensing our presence, left the trail and would have become entangled with the airplane had I not grabbed at Nugget's harness and steered him back on course. Susan, startled by our presence, surprised me. I had expected a tongue-lashing for touching her famous dog. Instead, she apologized for not paying closer attention, then disappeared into the swirling snow. Jim got the photo he was looking for, and we quickly flew off.

CHRIS AND JEFF left Koyuk later than we did. As they were flying across the ice near Golovin, heading toward White Mountain, the horizon faded from view, swallowed up in another ground blizzard. With no landmarks to follow, Chris immediately attempted to set the Cub down onto the ice. Unfortunately, the left wingtip landed first.

Chris says he didn't hear the steel V-brace crossbars in front of him being torn loose and he didn't feel the jagged knife-like edges slicing off most of his scalp. Nor did he feel the bones in an ankle and a wrist snap as pieces of the Cub tore loose and slammed into his body while the airplane careened across the ice.

It was over in seconds. The smell of death was close at hand. Silence and white surrounded them. Jeff, in the back seat, hadn't fared much better than Chris. His jaw had shattered against the back of the front seat. Neither man can remember getting out of the destroyed Cub that moments before had been Chris's pride and joy.

Through pain and confusion, they dug into the winter gear stuffed into the rear compartment of the Cub. "Chris, you gotta help me here," Jeff remembers saying at the time. Jeff also recalls that Chris, trying to maintain a grasp on reality despite his severe injuries, kept repeating: "You're Jeff Schultz and I'm Chris McDonnell. We're photographing the Iditarod race." Even in their state of shock, they managed to assemble a winter camp of sorts.

ROBERT SERVICE SAID IT FIRST. Strange things happen in the land of the midnight sun. Were it not for Maggie

Olson's birthday party, Chris and Jeff might never have survived their ordeal on the ice.

Wade Charles, another Iditarod Air Force pilot, told me how this part of the drama then unfolded. Wade says a Bering Air pilot flying out of Nome was the first to zero in on the emergency locator transmitter that automatically activated when the plane crashed. The transmitter was sending its screeching life-and-death pleas up into the ionosphere to the satellite that relayed the message into the rescue system, a message picked up by the pilot through Nome radio.

However, it was Jeff's hand-held VHF radio that really saved their butts. The emergency locator transmitter gave the system their approximate location. But Jeff was on the air with his little radio, sending out a repeated message: "Mayday. Mayday. This is Piper Super Cub 7685 Delta. We have crash-landed on Golovin Bay 5 miles beyond Golovin towards White Mountain. Pilot Chris McDonnell and passenger Jeff Schultz. We have injuries. We need snow-machines to come from Golovin to rescue us. Please help."

The Bering Air pilot answered Jeff's pleas over the radio and established a direct link to the crash site, but not until Jeff had exhausted a full set of batteries and replaced them with batteries meant for his cameras. When Jeff and Chris finally heard the airplane overhead through the blowing snow that was obliterating the evening sky, it was as if an angel had found them. The angel was a pilot named Will Vacendak.

Meanwhile in Golovin, folks were celebrating Maggie Olson's birthday. Maggie's son, Donny, who is a doctor, had flown into town earlier that day with other family members for the occasion. Wade Charles also was at the birthday party when the talk between the Bering Air pilot and Jeff came over the radio scanner. Maggie got on the radio; her family runs Olson Air and she knew Will, the Bering Air pilot.

Will gave Maggie the map coordinates of the downed plane, based on readings from his GPS (global positioning system) unit. Donny Olson had a hand-held GPS unit on the dashboard of the plane he had flown to Golovin to attend his mom's party. Someone was dispatched to retrieve the instrument while a search party was organized. The effort soon involved a medical team consisting of one doctor, one dentist, and one veterinarian. One of the party-goers was veterinarian Karin Schmidt, who rummaged through her supplies for any useful items. Then Donny, Karin, and a dentist who happened to be in town assembled an emergency medical kit at the Golovin clinic to take to the crash site.

His GPS unit firmly in hand, Donny Olson led the hastily formed ground search party out onto the ice on snowmachines. The crash site was about 5 miles away, and they knew it was going to be tough to find in the blinding snow and growing darkness. Will continued to fly above the crash site, assuring Chris and Jeff that help was on the way.

"Could you make some kind of a light?" Will asked the injured men over the radio. Such a beacon would help guide the searchers to them. Jeff found the airplane's catalytic engine heater and a can of Blazo, but his matches wouldn't burn. Chris found his lighter, dumped another slug of gas on the heater, and lit it. Chris and Jeff spotted the lights of the search party approaching on the ground just as the searchers saw the light at the airplane. Will watched from the air. When the dim flickering specks below him converged, Will banked over hard and headed to Nome.

FOR CHRIS AND JEFF, rescue came none too soon. They were in no condition to care for themselves through the long night to come. Wade recalls that the rescue party and the injured men arrived in Golovin about 11 P.M. Donny Olson could see that Chris and Jeff needed to get to an Anchorage hospital immediately. Maggie called for help, and a pilot flying a twin-engine plane carrying life-sustaining medical equipment was dispatched from Nome to Golovin.

Donny Olson and Mike Owens, a village health care worker, got aboard with the injured men to render aid during the 500-mile flight to Anchorage. The wind had eased somewhat by then, but fog had settled in and the snow was beginning to come straight down. By morning, 16 inches would accumulate. The flight went fine, however, and Chris and Jeff eventually recovered from their injuries. But if they hadn't been found when they were, the little white Super Cub with the red trim would have been the only clue to the location of their bodies. If ever a miracle happened, one surely took place that day near Golovin.

7   Hard Times

Al Lewis is not the only Iditarod Air Force pilot who has taken the trouble to name his airplane. Airline captain Mike Koskovich has flown *Blackbird*, a Cessna 180, off and on for years, helping out with the race. *Alaska Traveler* is what John Norris calls the 180 he flies along the trail. Jim Robertson, another professional pilot associated with the race, calls his plane *S.E.E.* (for Single Engine Emergency). Surveyor Floyd Tetpon, who usually flies the race marshal around, seems to refer to his plane as "Son of a Bitch" a great deal of the time. Educator Richard Burmeister, who has also seen the race from the back runners of a sled and has published a book of poems about his feelings along the trail, flies *Sweet Pea*. The pet name for my own Super Cub is *Baldy Bluebird*. But the name that stands out along the trail is Al Lewis's *Hard Times*. He hadn't intended to call it that, but once you know a little more about Al, you'll understand how it came to be.

Pilots are notorious for telling hair-raising tales of flying experiences, and Al tells more tales than most. Aviation is not always terror-filled, but everyone seems to want to hear "war stories." When things get slow, pilots everywhere are only too willing to spice things up. One thing is certain: as a pilot, you're always in the thick of things. This is true whether you're dropping bombs in a war zone, blasting off from Cape Canaveral in the space shuttle, or simply trying to find your way through Rainy Pass in marginal weather or picking up a veterinarian with a sick dog. The premise doesn't change. The person at the controls is definitely front and center. And Al loves to be the center of attention.

Perhaps it's living so close to danger that makes pilots relish every moment. And maybe that's why many pilots go out of their way to pull off pranks and bend the rules. Life is too temporary to be taken too seriously. Unless, of course, you work for the FAA.

Ostensibly to save us from ourselves, the Federal Aviation Administration has gotten deeper and deeper into the Iditarod race each year. Where pre-race meetings used to be casually held in someone's garage or living room over a few beers, they are now held in formal meeting rooms and attended by everyone involved with the race—including the federal government. The Iditarod pilots have grudgingly learned to live with the FAA's spot inspections (known as ramp checks). But Al once got around this ceremony.

At the time of the 1991 race, Al was in the process of refurbishing his entire bird, a Cessna 180. The insides (fabric, seats, instruments, you name it) had been stripped out. Wires were hanging everywhere. Panels had been taken out, exposing parts of an airplane most people never see. The doors didn't want to latch. Most of the paint had been removed. On any sales lot, this would have been one of those fixer-uppers that make even the most gullible keep walking.

But Al likes the race as much as anyone and didn't want to miss out. To be legal, he knew he needed a seat, at least one set of controls, an altimeter, an airspeed indicator, and a compass, plus the engine instruments. So he re-installed what he needed and headed for race headquarters at McGrath, a hand-held radio at his side.

TWO THINGS TURN HEADS in aviation: beautiful airplanes, and piles of junk that are somehow still in the air. Al's craft qualified in at least half those categories when he touched down and pulled up in front of race headquarters.

As if that weren't enough, this comedian of the trail decided at the last moment to take a can of black spray paint and write in 2-foot-high letters on both sides of his plane, HARD TIMES.

This was good for a laugh and made quite an impression on all who saw it—including the people from the FAA, who showed up after most everyone had tied down for the night.

The government boys were making their first inspections early the next morning as the Iditarod pilots pre-flighted their birds for the day's activities. *Hard Times* was nowhere to be seen. Although questions were asked during the ensuing days, no one seemed to know anything about its whereabouts. Eventually the race, and the FAA, moved on. Almost miraculously, *Hard Times* appeared back on the flight ramp, looking just as ragged as when it disappeared.

"Oh, I just moved it down onto the river ice," Al said. "I knew those government guys wouldn't walk very far."

When this undisputed trail charlatan gets going on a story, it's a virtual guarantee you'll laugh until your sides ache. But Al has a grim side too. The stories of the grief his unit took in Vietnam can also make you ache, but in a different way. Most of his buddies died in front of his eyes. Death hovered constantly about him. In his entire Vietnam tour of duty, Al himself didn't even suffer a scratch that would qualify him for some R & R. When times get tough, humor can be a pretty good ally.

8 Eagle Island Honeymoon

Incidents, as the FAA likes to refer to aviation mishaps, become common facts of life where the airplane takes the place of the automobile, as it does in most of Alaska. In a land with few roads, and filled with people who insist on living out that other American dream—the one with the cabin in the woods overlooking a lake or stream—lots of little airplane "incidents" are bound to happen. "Fender benders" would be a better term, because that's what you would call them if a car was involved. However, with an airplane, you might think of it as having a Rolls Royce in your driveway when it comes to the expense of fixing even the smallest ding. Let a friend borrow your Rolls to help out with a dog race, and you begin to get the picture.

Take, for example, Tommy Likos's "incident" in 1993 on the Yukon River at the Eagle Island checkpoint. The borrowed Rolls was Bert Hanson's Cessna 206. Add Cupid to the picture and you'll see that events along the Iditarod Trail are never uncomplicated.

Bert, a former Iditarod chief pilot, had decided to take the trip to Nome that year hanging on to the handles of a dog sled. He let Tommy use his airplane to help with the race. Bert is a captain with Reeve Aleutian Airlines. Tommy, once a Navy aircraft carrier pilot, now flies professionally out of Honolulu. Bert and Tommy are peers in every sense of the word, and best friends to boot. Perhaps the big difference that year was that Bert was married, with five kids; Tommy was single.

The healthy-looking tan that Tommy brought to the race did nothing to detract from his already good bachelor looks and free-wheeling spirit. If there was a party going on, it was almost certain Tommy would be one of the last to stagger home. Of course, Bert hadn't yet introduced him to that tall, slim, long-haired logistics volunteer, Pat Plunkett. When Tommy and Pat finally met in Nome at the end of the race that year, Cupid's arrow went straight to its mark and the two of them were soon inseparable.

WITH THE RACE OVER, it was time for the least glamorous phase of being a volunteer Iditarod pilot. This involves the jobs that need doing on the way back down the trail. The powers-that-be call it "back-sweeping."

"Would you mind on your way home stopping in Cripple (or some equally out-of-the-way place) and picking up the camping gear that was left there?" is how it usually starts out.

It's hard for a pilot to say no, even if he has already spent a week or more in Nome awaiting calm weather for a quick flight home. Thanks to commercial jets, everyone else is usually already home–including the dogs.

Tommy was asked to help clean up the checkpoint at Eagle Island on his flight home. When Tommy headed down the trail, he carried a tall, slim, long-haired passenger decked out in a beaver fur vest. About the time this romantic couple reached the area of the lodge at White Mountain, less than an hour out of Nome, the flying conditions evidently became "very poor." So they landed. Three days later, they finally pushed on to Eagle Island.

The landing in the snow on the Yukon River at Eagle Island was routine, but as Tommy taxied up the snow-packed track toward the parking area, the 206 slid off the frozen trail and into deep snow, where it incurred a "prop strike." (I believe that's what the FAA called it.) In plain English, the propeller was dinged up.

A series of radio messages followed between Tommy at Eagle Island and owner Bert Hanson in Anchorage, who located a replacement prop in Nome. Pilot Jim Cook flew the prop in his twin-engine Cessna 310 to Unalakleet, where another pilot took the prop the rest of the way to Eagle Island in a smaller craft, one that could land in the snow.

But the story was far from over for Jim Cook as he prepared to fly back to Nome. Leaving Unalakleet, he elected to use the shorter ice-covered gravel runway to take advantage of strong winds from the east. He didn't reckon on blowing snow blinding him at the last moment, causing him to hit an ice berm, which sheared off the nose wheel. The pricey 310 dropped onto the frozen runway, destroying both engines. (Jim carried insurance, so by Iditarod standards, his "gift" to the sled dog race didn't count.)

MEANWHILE, TOMMY AND PAT were stranded once again in a cozy romantic cabin. While the new propeller was being found and delivered, big flakes of snow continued to fill the Yukon River valley. When the new propeller finally arrived, the "honeymooners" reluctantly closed up the cabin and the checkpoint. It was time to head home.

On the takeoff run, the heavily loaded 206 wallowed in snow that had accumulated on the river to a depth of several feet. Several mile-long takeoff attempts had to be aborted. The plane just wouldn't go airborne. Finally Pat and some of the gear were put aboard another plane, and Tommy managed to scramble out of there alone.

In Minnesota later that year, Tommy, the confirmed bachelor, said "I do" to Pat, before a church full of disbelieving friends. His "best man" was a woman.

As for Bert, he had made a "gift" to the Iditarod cause that did indeed count. The timing of the Eagle Island "incident" was unfortunate because the Iditarod's insurance package for volunteer aircraft didn't come into being until the next race. It seems that the propeller damage turned out to include a bent crankshaft and a damaged engine that needed an overhaul after its tough times on the island. The receipts for Tommy's "incident" accumulated to something over $25,000. But on the bright side, Tommy and Bert are still best friends.

9 Student Pilot

The Iditarod Trail territory is not your typical training area for student pilots. There are no section lines or road junctions to serve as guideposts for carrying out airplane maneuvers with some semblance of precision. Emergency facilities are few and far between. Your compass can play crazy games with you this far north, and cross-country flights are definitely not practice runs. In fact, the Iditarod Trail is about as far from being a normal practice area as you can find in aviation.

But if you want to practice takeoffs and landings on very short fields; if you want to practice reading a sectional chart because your life depends on it; if you want to try mountain flying that offers downdrafts and squirrelly winds–then you probably couldn't find a better place to do it. Add the cold of an arctic winter and you begin to see what kind of gal Kathy (Mackey) Smith was when she was flying the trail while still a student pilot during the early years of the race. Raised in a gold-mining settlement somewhere north of Unalakleet, Kathy is from the same stock as the pioneer women who accompanied the covered wagons across the country to settle Oregon and California.

Kathy looked back on her Iditarod adventures during a conversation with me in her small cabin home in Wasilla.

"We were about 900 percent involved with the race," she said, referring to her husband at that time, Dick Mackey, who won the 1978 Iditarod. "Dick was in it and we had two kids at home and a dog lot to feed. So my hands were pretty full."

Kathy, now a shapely, dark-haired grandmother, nodded toward the airplane tied down outside the kitchen window. "Flying had always, just naturally, been a part of my life," she said. The landing strip was little more than a cut through the brush and trees.

It was hard for me to imagine anyone volunteering to help in the Iditarod while still a student pilot. Perhaps for folks born and raised under frontier conditions, such remarkable actions are the norm.

"The airplane seemed the most natural thing to do because I had to be home every night" to tend to the kids, Kathy said. "I couldn't stay out on the trail like the other volunteers."

"But Larry made it fun!" she added with a smile. Kathy gives Larry Thompson credit for everything she learned about flying, even though this longtime Iditarod volunteer wasn't her official instructor. "His teaching methods were a bit unorthodox," she said, then quickly added: "But Larry is the best pilot I've ever flown with or been around."

Somehow Kathy managed to survive her mistakes,

which were plenty. The Pacer she started out with happened to be the very first one off the Piper assembly line. The Pacer is a short plane, hard to control and prone to ground-looping (going into an out-of-control turn on the ground). The Pacer eventually became too small for the loads she and Dick hauled as they became more immersed in the race. They replaced the Pacer with a Cessna 180. The Pacer had been a tough plane to handle along the Iditarod Trail, but it was the Cessna that really began to get Kathy into trouble.

"I was green as a gourd in the 180," she said.

KATHY DID MOST OF HER Iditarod flying in the hundred-mile stretch between Anchorage and the checkpoint at Rainy Pass Lodge on Puntilla Lake, in the Alaska Range. It's a magnificent route, presenting a pilot with much of the majesty of the Alaskan landscape and its wildlife. On a windless day, with the magenta glow of the late afternoon March sun casting long pink shadows over the land, the country takes on a mellow appearance that can be misleading. Moose can be seen in the willows or on the side of Sleeping Lady, the 3,000-foot mountain that reclines in all her lovely nakedness for the people of Anchorage to see every day from across Cook Inlet. For a pilot, the smooth, silky air can be spellbinding.

On the flight from Anchorage, a flyer sees the land spreading out on the other side of the inlet, rising slowly to meet the distant mountains. It is the drainage of the same peaks that include Mount McKinley. The swampy land becomes foothills as you reach Finger Lake, where the snow can pile in over your head and wind can make the frozen surface a mess of berms and drifted ruts. But when it's calm and you're the first one there on new snow, the skis just float you into the landing.

Flying on from Finger Lake, Happy River comes into view almost at once. The river is a difficult part of the trail for the mushers, but from the air, it looks like a nice winding trail through spruce and birch.

Climbing steadily into the mountains now toward Puntilla Lake and Rainy Pass Lodge, a pilot can see the trail below as it ascends between the rising hills and over some ponds, while trees become more and more sparse. Then you're at the lodge—a good place for a cup of coffee and a chance to hear the latest on conditions at the pass if you are pushing on into the Interior.

The horse corrals near the lodge seem strangely out of place in the middle of these mountains, but then you remember that this is primarily a hunting lodge and not just another checkpoint for the Iditarod. The horses here work for their keep. They are pressed into service each fall to get hunters and guides up into the 7,000-foot peaks that tower over the valley.

Dall sheep find shelter in these mountains, but they are hard to spot against the snow. Moose tracks are evident, and caribou passages can be seen as well. Scrub willows, the last of the trees at this elevation, grow along the isolated creeks. A fox lingers along the trail, and you wonder if he has been reduced by the cold to making his living by eating the feces of his larger, better-fed cousins who pull sleds up the trail each March. For a downed pilot, keeping warm here would be a grim undertaking.

THIS IS THE LAND that Kathy got to know well as a student pilot, the land where she had some lively adventures. On one memorable occasion—in poor light, her plane heavily loaded with dog food—Kathy couldn't quite see the touch-down area on Puntilla Lake in front of Rainy Pass Lodge. Her approach was too low, and her airspeed was too slow.

Trying to get down "exactly on the spot," as she knew Larry would expect, she stalled the aircraft as she came in for the landing. The 180 was already falling off on one wing and was headed toward disaster. But because she had mis-judged her altitude and was lower than she thought she was, one of the plane's skis contacted the snow before the 180 could go out of control. She was lucky.

"Looking back," she said, "everything I did was wrong on that landing."

Another time, she was asked to fly from Anchorage to Rainy Pass Lodge to fetch a load of dogs.

"It was snowing hard at the time," she said. "Larry was already there."

Kathy waited for the snowstorm to subside before ven-turing out. As she landed at the lodge, Larry was flying out on his way back to Anchorage. Before she could get the dogs on board and follow him, another snow squall came blowing in. Coffee time in the lodge. Conditions got worse.

Time was running out on her flight plan, which pilots file so that everyone knows their route and planned arrival

times. She radioed to Finger Lake and arranged with someone to call Anchorage Flight Service to cancel her flight
plan. She would have to fly out later, when the weather
improved.

But something went wrong in communications. No one
closed out the flight plan. But Kathy didn't know this. And
neither did Larry—now back in Anchorage, and expecting
Kathy to land there shortly.

At the lodge, some time later, the people inside heard
an airplane overhead, in the snowstorm. They couldn't
believe that someone would try to fly in such conditions.
There was no doubt in Kathy's mind that it was Larry.

Larry landed his plane. Not even taking the time to
shut the engine down, he stomped over in his narrow-toed
cowboy boots to where Kathy and the others were waiting.

"You planning on homesteading this place or what?" he
snarled, obviously burning under the collar.

"If you want to get home, follow me—NOW!"

And so, off into the white they went, Kathy barely able
to keep track of the strobe light on Larry's tail.

The weather was a lot better in Anchorage, but Larry's
mood was not.

"As soon as we had the airplanes tied down, he proceeded to chew me a new ass," Kathy said.

"When you fly in the bush, you always tell someone
when you change your plans!" he roared at her.

"But I closed my flight plan through Finger Lake when
the snow got so bad," she stammered.

"You did?"

Larry is not the kind of person to be subdued very

often. This time he was. He had been worried when Kathy hadn't returned, so he flew back through the storm to find her, without thought for his own safety. His anger had been out of concern for her.

"When the flying day was over, all was forgiven and forgotten," Kathy said. "Then it was time to head for the tavern. That's when Larry made it fun."

10 Cold

Word came filtering down from headquarters: "No one has to start their engines until the temperature gets up to 30 below." This announcement came as a relief for a greenhorn Iditarod Air Force pilot like myself. It was officially 47 below zero that morning in McGrath. I had been up since before six in the cold darkness getting my Super Cub ready to fly. Every bootstep crunched under my weight as I moved about the plane in the snow, and the hair froze inside my nose as I breathed deeply from inside the hood of my down parka. I had to remove my mittens, but I made sure that the fingered gloves underneath stayed put.

I'd flown in minus 25-degree temperatures before and had learned to enjoy the stability of the Super Cub in the cold air. Normally the 160 horses under the Cub's cowling leap to the task of getting us airborne. But this time they didn't want to respond. I held the throttle full on–hard–anticipating the acceleration and the feeling of lifting off into the clear, cold air. Instead, the engine quietly died. I coasted to a stop on skis, crawled out, and wrestled the plane to the side of the runway. I got the engine started again and taxied back to the tie-down area, my mind filled with unanswered questions. That's when the welcome news came that we didn't have to fly until it got up to 30 below.

As you read these chapters about the air force, you won't see much mention of the nuts and bolts of day-to-day operations in severe winter weather. But you can be sure the pilots are very aware of the special requirements of flying under arctic conditions. It becomes second nature to keep the oil warm when the plane is on the ground; to use additives for keeping moisture out of the fuel; to clear snow off the wings and windshields. Arctic winds can blow powdery snow into a plane's interior, affecting its weight and balance. It's almost as important to heat the inside of the plane as it is to heat the engine under conditions of extreme cold. Instrument knobs can pull right off the panel when they are frozen; frost inside instruments can cause them to malfunction. And then there are the clothes a pilot needs to stay warm, such as the cumbersome "bunny boots." These are things taken for granted when pilots volunteer themselves and their planes to help out with the world's most famous dog race.

The Iditarod Air Force now has an official pilot's handbook, a big change from the free-and-easy early days. First off, a prospective volunteer learns from the handbook that you can no longer do your student pilot training along the trail. Besides the FAA requirements (such as annual inspection, equipment list, medical certificate, etc.), the Iditarod Trail Committee insists a pilot hold a commercial license. The committee also wants a minimum of 1,000 hours of flying time, with 500 of it in Alaska, 100 hours of winter experience within the past two years, and another 100 hours on skis if your airplane is so equipped. The State of Alaska requires you to have full survival gear on board—and foolish is the pilot who doesn't. This means sleeping bag, food, shelter, engine heater, fuel for the heater, snowshoes, a firearm with plenty of ammunition, and an ax. The Iditarod folks also want you to have a snow shovel, ice screws, wing and windshield covers, and plenty of tie-down lines to keep your plane from being blown away on the ground. If you're hauling a passenger and his gear along in your Cub, you're lucky to find space for your own toothbrush.

BACK ON THAT EXTRA-COLD DAY in McGrath, I had managed to taxi to the tie-down area, my brain trying to fathom why the engine of my perfectly airworthy Super Cub would quit on takeoff. Several mechanics' opinions later, trail veteran George Murphy came up with the answer, and the solution. He showed me how to affix duct tape (called "hundred-mile-an-hour tape" by pilots of fabric-covered airplanes) to the cowling to reduce the amount of cold air coming in on the engine. "Just leave your carb heat on when you take off," he told me. "You're getting too much supercooled air into the engine and it's starving for gas."

On my next takeoff attempt, the Cub leaped into the air like it meant business. I'll have to admit to some misgivings about the whole thing, because my insides were churning as I looked down on the frozen muskeg and spikes of spruce waiting to greet me if George was wrong. He wasn't.

11 Media Mania

The few telephones that are found in villages along the race route are put to full use by reporters, with dateline stories going to press almost as they occur. Unlike the early years of the race, when media attention couldn't even be bought, today even Nome's little KNOM radio station hires a plane for reporting live along the trail. And every reporter wants the latest scoop. But don't expect to get it from the Iditarod Air Force; the pilots are too busy. Once the race starts, activity is almost a blur, and the last thing on their minds is answering questions from the media.

What the pilots really care about are such things as a broken generator at Cripple or a dog that needs hauling out of Rohn—things they can do something about. Once the race passes through a checkpoint, the pilots are concerned with shuttling veterinarians and other personnel and their gear on ahead. Then it's cleanup, pack-up time, and the push is on again as the whole operation moves up the trail. Confusing? It can get that way in a hurry, but the pilots who volunteer every year seem to take it in stride. What they can fill you in on, though, are the latest shenanigans along the trail.

Even in the heat of the race, no one is immune from pilot pranks–least of all the media. ABC and ESPN have done an exceptional job covering the race over the years. There are countless others out there as well, including reporters from local TV, newspapers, radio stations, and magazines. All are clamoring for something unique to tempt their audiences.

One of the pilots reported he had heard that ice hockey great Wayne Gretzky was in Nome at the end of the race, "buying dogs like crazy."

"No doubt," he added with the flair of someone who is in the know, "Wayne is planning to add the Iditarod to his list of accomplishments."

The female reporter who scooped that story and actually got it published was livid. Her credibility was shattered! But to the group of pilots at the Board-Of-Trade Saloon, it was hilarious.

In the town of McGrath, McGuires is the place to be after hours when the race goes through the area each March. An Anchorage TV station was setting up lights, sound, and cameras in McGuires one night for a report. The air force guys, having tied their planes down for the night, were there, ready for the big show. As the clock ticked down the last seconds before the cameras were to start rolling, most of those in attendance at the tavern were feeling little pain. The wife of one of the mushers, who was supposed to be out on the trail as a volunteer, had ended up that evening on the lap of one of the pilots. Everybody was laughing and having a great time. About then, pilot Danny Davidson walked over to the TV crew and grabbed the reporter by the arm.

"Hey, the story you want is over here!" he said as he pulled the reporter along to where the clowning was in full swing just as the appointed air time arrived.

Having someone else's wife on your lap is one thing. Being seen on the evening news that way is another matter entirely. All the pilots thought the TV broadcast was a riot, except for one. He raced for the phone.

"Honey," he said when his wife answered, "do me a big favor and get on the next flight to McGrath and bring my heavy parka. It's really cold here, and I've sure been missing you!" She made the flight, and missed seeing him on the news.

Unbeknownst to the wife of the musher, her husband had made it into McGrath earlier than expected and had settled in for a few hours of much-needed rest at someone's house. He caught only a glimpse of the evening news, but it was more than enough. Not everyone can take a joke. Two years later, the musher and his wife divorced. Well . . . maybe the TV broadcast wasn't the whole cause.

IT'S NOT CERTAIN who got the idea to stage the liquor raid on ABC's suite of rooms at the lodge in Unalakleet. We do know that it was pilot Al Lewis, the trail charlatan, who donned a badge and an official-looking leather jacket, posing as the village public safety officer. Al knew that personal consumption of booze was legal in Unalakleet, even though you couldn't buy or sell the stuff in town. But he was betting that the ABC crowd wouldn't be so sure. The ploy worked.

Al barged through the door and into a room full of open bottles. Very loudly, with a straight face, he demanded the same attention that the ABC celebrities and officials, who were seated around the room, get when they go on the air.

"What do you mean drinking here? You know this is a dry village! Alcohol is illegal!" he roared while snatching up bottle after bottle as he made his way around the room.

A woman somewhere in the back of the room tried to counter his offensive with one of her own. In a very loud whisper, she said:

"Don't you know you are disturbing one of Alaska's premier bush pilots who's trying to get some rest back here?"

She was talking about Tony Oney Sr., who flies ABC personnel along the trail. But she was making her case before the wrong audience. The pilots and Tony had a long history of whooping it up together along the trail.

Ignoring the woman's remark, Al kept scooping up bottles as he headed for the door—a rapidly developing case of the snickers almost beating him there.

Once outside the room, the prank was in the open. The other pilots, who silently had their ears glued to the door and walls outside as they listened to Al's performance, were laughing uncontrollably. The bounty was distributed to all at hand. Even the ABC crew had to admit, at a later party in Nome, that it was a pretty good joke. But at the time, they didn't think so.

IDITAROD PHOTOGRAPHER JIM BROWN likes to tell the story about a reporter who didn't need anyone to fool her. She did it herself.

This reporter-photographer was assigned to do a feature on the Iditarod for a large publication back East. She arrived in Anchorage a few days before the race and proceeded to outfit herself with a complete set of arctic gear: mukluks, fur parka, mitts–the works! She was quite splendid-looking.

Then she rented a winterized motor home for the entire month of March. The gun went off in Anchorage for the start of the race, and the mushers headed out of town, followed by Arctic Lady. In Wasilla, she decided to top off her fuel tanks for the long haul ahead.

"How do you get to the trail?" she enthusiastically asked the gas station attendant.

"Just go back to the light and head out Knik Road. It'll take you right there," he said, not completely understanding the full meaning of her enthusiasm.

The reporter, for her part, had no idea that her story of a lifetime, the one she planned to cover in person along the trail all the way to Nome, was about to come to a screeching halt in less than 15 miles. The Knik Road, as everyone in Alaska knows, dead-ends somewhere out in the Point

MacKenzie Agricultural Project. The trail leaves the road at the Knik Bar, goes across Knik Lake, and heads toward the frozen swamps and heavy timber, where it eventually hits the Yentna River on its way to Skwentna. It's the last road for the next thousand miles.

12 Fire

"Anybody on? Is anybody on here? This is 04 Foxtrot! I've got fire and smoke in my cabin. I'm putting her down."

"This is Reagan. Where are you?"

"I just left Cripple going northwest! The GPS says 64-11.68 north and 155-27.82 west."

"Got it! Be there ASAP!"

NOTHING IN AVIATION, other than a wing coming off in flight, will get your attention more quickly than a fire on board.

Eric Johnson was on his way to Galena by way of Kaltag. This tall, handsome pilot with the western drawl had flown out of Cripple about 11 A.M. His wife, Linda, was aboard, and the plan was to drop Linda at Kaltag to help the Iditarod communications people while Eric went on to Galena for other flight duties.

"I just drew a line between Cripple and Kaltag," Eric told me. "There isn't anything between the two except brush." Then the excitement of the event, nearly two years old, came back into his voice: "The fire actually burst out the engine cowling, scorching the windshield and the door frame!"

The area of Cripple is no place to set down a burning plane. The checkpoint itself is cold, dreary, uncomfortable. Only 60 miles downstream from Ophir and on the same picturesque little Innoko River, Cripple seems the antithesis of the warmth and homeyness that Ophir represents. The land west of Cripple, where Eric was piloting his burning airplane, is no better. On that day, the temperature outside was 40 below zero.

As soon as fire and smoke filled the cockpit, Eric and Linda looked for a place to put the plane down. That's when Eric got on the radio, hoping to let someone know where to start looking for them. There were only trees and brush for miles in any direction except for a tiny, narrow opening of snow along a small creek. Linda grabbed sleeping bags and coats to brace in front of them for the stop that was to come. They knew the wings were going to be sheared off the plane when it hit the opening.

Just then another white patch caught Eric's eye. It was dead ahead and oblong. An open strip! The strip was a couple of thousand feet long. The landing on the powdery, 18-inch-deep snow was easy. As they slid to a stop about midpoint down the strip, Eric shut down the engine. The fire went out.

You can imagine their surprise when, moments later, in

untracked whiteness, a four-wheel-drive truck pulled up to them. It was the winter watchman from a nearby gold mine whose airstrip they had invaded. Winter emergencies are about the only acceptable reason for an unannounced landing at a gold mine in Alaska; otherwise expect to look down the barrel of a gun. Gold miners tend to be from that school that shoots first and asks questions later. Evidently winter watchmen come from a different school. This fellow exchanged greetings with Eric and Linda and offered them a warm place to stay.

Eric got back on the radio and contacted Reagan Russey, another veteran of the trail, who by this time was flying overhead. It was a good feeling for Eric to hear a friendly voice and be able to report that he and Linda were fine.

Eric still wanted to know what caused the fireball, of course. He opened the cowling on the engine, fearing he would find a molten mass of wires, meaning a major repair job. He was pleasantly surprised to find only that a winter baffle had come loose. The baffle had rubbed a hole in a gas injector line. The gas had ignited on the manifold. Fortunately the supercooled air had prevented what could have been a disaster. A tin wrap, a clamp, and some tape soon had Eric and Linda on their way once again.

PILOT DAVE ALBORN was another guy who received a hot surprise from his airplane. The setting was Nome, after the finish of the 1993 race. Every pilot in town was pinned down long after the last mushers had made it through the banquets held in their honor. Blizzards blowing out of the northeast refused to let any plane leave town, while the cold continued to plague any machinery that tried to move.

Everyone was anxious to get out of Nome as soon as possible. All the pilots were keeping their airplanes heated and at the ready in case a break came in the weather. Details are a bit sketchy on the near-fatal incident that occurred outside Olson's hangar.

"A fifty-thousand-dollar mistake!" is all that I could get out of Dave that evening—besides the wry smile.

Dave was chief pilot that year, so his time was spread pretty thin. As the story slowly came together, it seems that someone else had put the engine heater on the spiffy Cessna 185 that Dave was flying. Dave had come out to the airport to check on the heater, which this unnamed person had placed under the engine cowling earlier in the day.

To see if the oil in the pan was warming, Dave reached up to turn the prop through a revolution or two. It's an easy way to tell how the warming is going. It was hot all right— as were both magnetos, even though their switches were in the off position. How the throttle got left in the full-on position is still a mystery.

With his right hand, Dave grabbed the prop from behind on the left side of the airplane. He first looked into the cockpit, as any pilot does almost automatically, to see that the mags were in the off position. But the propeller had barely moved when the 185 roared to life, at full power, lunging against the tie-down ropes.

Dave was lucky to be behind the propeller. Otherwise he would have been chewed to bits by the three blades that went from zero to 2800 rpm in one second. The sudden start broke the tie-down rope on the left side, and the airplane lunged away. But still tethered by the right-side line, the plane swung out and away in an arc and proceeded to beat itself to death on the frozen snowbanks at the field. The disaster was over in fewer seconds than it takes to tell.

Miraculously, Dave wasn't even scratched, and none of the nearby planes were damaged. It could have been a double-doozy if both tie-downs had snapped. Insurance had just become part of the Iditarod package that year, but investigators started wrangling over the incident almost immediately. In the meanwhile, Dave took to using his little Piper PA-11. A year later, that was still the only plane he had.

13 Dogs on the Loose

A sled dog on the loose can cause considerable concern during the Iditarod. For a musher along the trail, it means disqualification if the dog can't be found and returned to its team. The Iditarod Air Force has been pressed into service more than once to locate dogs that invariably head back down the trail toward home rather than pushing on to Nome.

Several of us once searched the Farewell Burn for a dog that had gotten loose near Nikolai. The dog managed to evade everyone while he backtracked along the 93 miles of trail from Nikolai to Rohn. Someone saw the dog in the spruce trees that surround the little checkpoint cabin at Rohn, but he was too skittish to come to them.

The critter continued on his way toward Anchorage. Forty-eight miles later, having made it over the Alaska Range and past all the trailing racers, the dog met up with Joe Redington and his entourage, who were following up the trail behind the race. After covering nearly 150 miles on his own, the dog felt hungry enough to come close to Joe. For this dog that had known such a brief spurt of freedom, it was a big mistake. Joe fed him, then hitched him to his sled. When the sled reached Nome, Joe had the only dog there to have covered the entire Iditarod plus an extra 300 miles.

CATCHING A LOOSE DOG can be an embarrassing experience, as Bill Mayer learned. It happened during his favorite kind of afternoon, calm and lovely. He was leisurely flying out of Anchorage to help with cleaning up the back trail on the eastern side of the Alaska Range. Bill Kramer, who was handling the Anchorage end of the chief pilot's job, had already been flying the trail, on the lookout for a loose dog. The two pilots made radio contact.

"Just keep flying up the river," Kramer said to Mayer. "There's a loose dog heading home somewhere between Yentna Station and Skwentna. Maybe you'll be able to spot it."

Mayer, a good-humored Anchorage cardiologist who has been flying the trail since 1990, gave an interesting reason for volunteering as an Iditarod pilot. In the questionnaire that asked pilots why they got involved in the race, Mayer listed: "Late afternoon on a calm day." Most everyone who flies the trail knows the feeling. It comes flooding over you when the mountains and landscape are aglow in the reddish orange of the winter sun; when the airplane feels as though it's suspended above the terrain or sliding through silky liquid, with the engine noise trailing far off somewhere behind your thoughts. There isn't a better time to be in the air.

Sure enough, on just such an afternoon, Mayer's drifting thoughts were suddenly brought back into focus when he saw a dog heading down the river.

"Hey, Bill!" Mayer called to Kramer on their Iditarod frequency. "I think I've found it!"

"Where?"

"Just north of where the Susitna and the Yentna come together."

"Great!" Kramer answered back. "You land somewhere below it and head it off. I'll fly your way and land above you. We can't let it get past us! See you in a few minutes."

"But there's a couple of snowmachines already chasing it," Mayer said.

"That's even better!" Kramer said. "If you miss it, have them run it down for you. I'll be there as soon as I can."

So Mayer landed his Cessna 185 on the river ice in fairly deep snow a quarter mile below the chase. He positioned himself out on the trail.

As the dog got closer, Mayer danced back and forth, arms outstretched, trying to calculate which way the dog might bolt at the last moment. The dog raced toward him. By lunging with everything he was worth, Mayer tackled the now-terrified dog in the deep snow beside the trail.

About then the snowmachines arrived on the scene. Kramer buzzed low overhead.

"What are you doing to our dog?" the snowmachiners cried in unison. Their excitement and loud voices were accentuated because of the hubbub of the roaring airplane overhead.

"Your dog?" Mayer replied in the same elevated voice. "I thought it was the lost sled dog we've been searching for."

"Hell no! We just turned him loose up the river a ways to give him some exercise."

Kramer could hardly see to land because of the tears his laughing caused when Mayer related the details by radio. The snowmachiners drove off in hot pursuit of the dog that wasn't lost. By this time, someone upriver had gotten hold of the correct dog and all was well once again. Mayer had had enough late-afternoon, sun-drenched Alaska wilderness for one day and headed back to his office in Anchorage.

SLED DOGS ON THE LOOSE aren't in a very safe situation. Relatively timid and accustomed to plenty of affection, a stray sled dog wandering into a village full of barking, half-wild, eat-anything critters can be in mortal danger. With sled dogs commonly worth thousands of dollars, the disappearance of a dog would be both a substantial monetary and emotional loss for a musher. And there would be hell to pay for any pilot responsible for losing a dog.

These were the thoughts turning in my head the day I flew into Nome from White Mountain with five dogs in the back seat and baggage compartment of my Cub. I was also carrying some important veterinary supplies, including blood samples. My hands were full, and there was no one to meet me when I landed on the sea ice in front of the visitor's center.

Nome has an ungodly volume of dogs even when the race isn't in town. Add thirty or so Iditarod finishing teams and it gets downright crowded. I carefully lifted each of the dogs out of my Cub and hooked them to the ski cables. The dogs were pretty docile, and the one with the injured leg had already won my heart. It seemed reasonable, at the time, to simply hook all the dogs together in single file and lead them up off the ice and onto the dog lot beside the center. That way, I had my other arm free to carry the vet samples.

Everything went OK until the injured fellow, last in the dog train, refused to climb the pressure ridge that had formed just offshore. In one simple twist of his head, he was free of his collar and standing on the ice while the others scrambled up onto the shore. So there I was, vet supplies under one arm, leading four dogs and a dangling collar, and only a hundred yards from a town overrun with dogs. An injured dog on the loose was definitely not in anyone's best interest.

With me and the dog train up on the rough shore ice and the "caboose dog" down on the smooth sea ice, my options were limited. So I did the best thing possible and did nothing. I sat down among the dogs I had control over and hoped for the best.

Sure enough, the injured fellow found his own route up to our level. Skittish and nervous with all the barking and commotion coming from town, he soon sniffed his way closer, lured by all the smooth talking I was doing to the other four. Finally he succumbed to the same scratching and petting the others were enjoying. When we got to the street, I commandeered some help from the first passerby, and it all ended up without the big-gun mushers who owned the dogs ever knowing the full tale.

14 Mean Streak

Cindy the Vet is all Bill Kramer can remember of her name. They were in his Cessna 185, hauling ten dogs back to Anchorage from one of the checkpoints, when a commotion in the back among the dogs got out of hand. Pilots usually take the time to cable the dogs in place before a flight. On this trip, Bill learned why.

A big black male, known to have a mean streak, was taking out his meanness on one of the other dogs. Usually a growl or two is all that happens between dogs on a flight. If they do get a bit rambunctious, a forward push on the yoke, to float them in the air a bit, settles them right down. This time though, from the sound of things, blood was going to be drawn.

Bill was looking for a place to put the plane down when Cindy said, "Forget it, Bill, let's just get them back to town. I'll stitch up whatever happens when we get there."

The other eight dogs, of course, figured they were next in line for a mauling. They began making their way forward over the rear seat and into the cockpit any way they could.

As Bill talked to the Lake Hood tower at Anchorage and made preparations to land, he was also trying to elbow the head of a dog coming between the two front seats. Cindy was frantically dividing her time between the dog Bill was fighting off and another frightened male, who was squirming his way up between the seat and the window on her side of the plane. That dog had already managed to get his head and shoulders into the cockpit when Bill told Cindy he was going to reach around behind her and get the dog by the tail and throw it into the back—but she would have to control the one whose head was now between them.

Just before they touched down, Bill grabbed for the tail and threw the dog backward with all the force he could muster. In carrying out this desperate maneuver, Bill got hold of more than the dog's tail. His thumb hooked a lock of Cindy's long blond curls and the cord to her headset. Cindy's head was jerked back violently, and her headset flew into the pile of snarling dogs. Hair was everywhere. Cindy's screams were barely audible above the fracas as the 185 set down on the runway.

Bill tried to apologize and soothe Cindy as he taxied the airplane while talking to ground control. By this time, the big black male had let go of his victim. All was quiet once again.

KATHY (MACKEY) SMITH, during her days as a student pilot along the trail, was once about to haul a load of dogs back to Anchorage when someone ran out to stop her.

"We have one that is dead," she was told. "They want to autopsy it in Anchorage. Think you could you take it along as well?"

The dogs in Kathy's plane were all aboard and settled down, and Kathy was ready to take off. But she said OK, she would take the dead dog with her. She regretted the decision only moments into the air.

There are a lot of things to understand about canines, whether they be house dogs or sled dogs, and one of those is pack mentality. You often hear of a pack of dogs chasing deer, or sometimes even attacking a child. The point is that dogs still have the wildness of the wolf buried within their genes. Get around a bunch of sled dogs that are about to be fed or hitched up for a morning's run, and you know the gene is not buried very deeply.

Perhaps it should have been obvious that if you put a piece of meat into an airplane loaded with thinly disguised wolves, you are going to have a dogfight. That's what happened when the dogs in Kathy's plane got wind of the dead animal. She reacted immediately. The plane was quickly back on the airstrip she had left only a few minutes before.

Was she any wiser for the experience?

"You bet!" Kathy answered before the question was even completely out.

15 Lost

The race had been plagued with weather problems almost from the start. More than once, the race was stopped because of the deep snows. The year was 1985. By the time the lead mushers reached the coast, a series of storms was coming in off the sea and rushing inland. There was little time to get braced between blows, and the strain was beginning to take its toll.

Up ahead, Norton Sound waited with the patience of a black widow spider for a musher unwary enough to set foot upon its frozen, yet wet, silky web. Libby Riddles took the gamble and ventured on out of Shaktoolik and into the storm that was sweeping in over the ice. It gave her a place in history because the daring move let her become the first woman to win the Iditarod.

Other mushers also ventured on and made it across that barren stretch of ice that can be as dangerous as anything along the trail. Farther back in the pack, though, four other mushers were not so fortunate. They had already spent one night together out in the storm on Norton Sound, and no one had heard from them since.

From Nome, chief pilot Les Reynolds had sent out a warning to the flyers of the Iditarod Air Force. He told them to get on the ground early and secure their planes. Another blow was due to slam into the area.

The wife of one of the four mushers came to Les, lines of concern etched in her face. Les asked if her husband, who was a surveyor, had a compass with him. He did. Les was relieved, because he then knew the likelihood of the four mushers wandering west toward the sea and onto a free-floating section of ice was nil. If they had lost the trail, they would play it safe and move to the east, where the ice would be the most secure.

A ground blizzard out over Norton Sound had been raging for most of the last twenty-four hours and was about to get worse. A second night of being stranded out there could spell disaster for the four mushers, and a search was organized.

In Nome, Donna Gentry climbed into Les's airplane with him and they headed for Koyuk, at the head of Norton Sound. Veterinarian Jim Leach, who was flying the trail, headed that way too. In Unalakleet, Danny Davidson was already firing up his Cessna 180 when Dave Alborn came running up to accompany him, and they too flew toward the scene. By this time, everyone along the trail had a gut feeling that something bad had happened to prevent the mushers from completing the 58 miles from Shaktoolik to Koyuk.

WITH DARKNESS APPROACHING, the searchers in the three airplanes had little time to find the mushers. The ground blizzard cut visibility just above the ice to almost zero–even though 50 feet in the air, the sky was clear. Winds pushing toward 40 knots made the flying tricky. The only way the people in the planes could see anything on the ice was by looking straight down. The three airplanes crisscrossed the general area of the trail. If the mushers had gone much off the trail, it would be next to impossible to find them.

Then Danny and Dave spotted some dark lumps in the snow, in a spot close to Koyuk and not very far east of the trail. A second pass confirmed that the lumps were half-buried sleds, but there was no sign of life. Danny radioed to Les and told him he was looking for a place to set down.

Risking it all, Danny lined up into the wind and let his plane find its own way to the ice the last 50 feet. Had anything been in Danny's path, his 180 would have been added to the growing list of planes already sacrificed to the Iditarod cause. The two other planes circled overhead as they made radio contact with some snowmachiners in Koyuk.

When Danny's plane came to a halt, Dave stayed with the craft to handle the controls while Danny tried to locate the mushers. He found them in their sleeping bags beside their sleds. Only one was able to unzip himself from his frozen bag unaided. By morning, it is likely they all would have been encased permanently inside their cocoons.

The blinding snow of the past twenty-four hours had driven so deeply into their clothing that they had all gotten wet. When they lost the trail, the surveyor knew enough to keep veering to the east so they wouldn't wander out on thin ice. They knew that eventually they would hit the shore, where they could simply turn west toward Koyuk. However, with the wet soaking into them, they decided it was safer to stop and wait for better weather before trying to figure out where they were. And here is where the controversy comes in.

These volunteer pilots had risked everything to find the mushers. When someone's wife comes to you with that worried look in her eyes, it is hard not to respond. Les and the others were sure that with another night out on the ice, the mushers could easily have become casualties of the race. But the mushers didn't see it that way.

Accepting aid along the trail is cause for disqualification. Only one of the four, the one whose wife was worried, had the courage to come forward afterward to offer his gratitude. The others tried to shrink into oblivion. The possibility of being disqualified scared them more than the possibility of not seeing another sunrise.

16 Payback at Sulatna

It's a grinding, cold 112 miles from Cripple and up out of the Innoko Valley and over the Ruby Hills to the Yukon, where the well-publicized seven-course dinner awaits the first musher to reach the big river. Sulatna Crossing is a good place to stop and rest before pushing the last 75 miles up over the hills. The little steel bridge that spans the Sulatna River seems strangely out of place in a land with no roads except the occasional "cat trails" punched out by Caterpillar-type tractors in gold-mining country.

Snow can be waist deep and more by the bridge as race time rolls around each March. The volunteer trail breakers on their snowmachines earn all the thanks they can get for punching through here on their way to intersect the cat trail that leads to Ruby and the Yukon. The fifteen or twenty parking spots for dog teams that they pack down near the bridge are greatly appreciated by both dogs and mushers when the teams finally arrive from Cripple.

The pilots, too, earned praise for their efforts at Sulatna Crossing in the years before it was eliminated as a stopover point, stockpiling straw, dog food, and other supplies the mushers asked for. The Sulatna Crossing landing doesn't require instruments, but Danny Davidson could have used a snow-depth gauge before he touched down one day on the trackless snow that covered the swamp by the bridge. Almost instantly, his 180 sank nearly out of sight into the sugary powder he had believed to be wind-packed snow.

Bruce Maroney was the first to fly to his aid.

"Don't land, Bruce!" Danny called over the radio. "Whatever you do—don't land!"

Sammy Maxwell was next on the scene, in his Super Cub. In Alaska, Cub drivers and their planes convey a stereotyped image of being able to do anything. And indeed, Cubs perform miraculous feats in the bush. With an ingrained attitude that "Cubs can get in and out of anywhere," a Cub pilot soon becomes invincible. Sammy was no stranger to this attitude. He knew he was going to land before he got there.

"Sammy, if you're missing even one piece of survival gear, go back and get it and then come on in," Danny warned from his buried cockpit. Only the wings and parts of the tail indicated to the two airplanes circling overhead that a plane was on the ground.

"I've got everything," Sammy answered as he skimmed over the surface on his touchdown. He nearly made the turnaround back into his own tracks before the little Cub, invincible as it may have seemed, sunk to a precarious tilt, its left wing nearly buried. Sammy's door was on the high side of the plane, so he was able to crawl out onto a ski and down into the nearly chest-deep snow. Danny would not be spending the night alone.

BRUCE WAS CIRCLING above the show. As a captain with Mark Air since 1977, Bruce knows his way around the radio airways, and he soon made contact with an Alaska Airlines flight outbound from Anchorage to a destination above the Arctic Circle. From their 30,000-foot perch, the crew members of the Alaska Airlines flight were better able to contact a group of trail breakers and tell them about the downed planes. Word was relayed to the stranded pilots that the trail breakers aboard their snowmachines were on the way.

Danny and Sammy floundered around in the snow, trying to organize their survival gear while waiting for help. In the six hours it took the snowmachines to wallow their way to the two pilots, other Iditarod flyers showed up above the scene, making so many "bombing runs" with food and supplies that Danny and Sammy figured they could have stayed for a year.

Finally they radioed to their comrades that beer was all they needed. "Forget the dried jerky!"

It was difficult to find all the stuff that was being dropped to them. When the packages landed, they would punch through the snow, just as the airplanes had done. With the momentum of the drop, the packages would then slide farther along beneath the crust, ending up in tall swamp grass that had been covered by the deep snow.

Danny and Sammy were like moles lifting the sod on a newly mowed lawn as they scurried around, breaking through the crust, searching for the dropped goods.

Along toward late afternoon, a faint buzzing sound told them that the trail breakers were coming near. The pilots still had plenty of time to get into position by the bridge abutments, where the reflecting sun had warmed the sugary snow into perfect snowball material. Instead of being welcomed with steaming cups of cocoa, the trail breakers were greeted with a volley of snowballs as they came across the bridge. Having a good time at the other group's expense has always been considered fair play along the trail. The cocoa came later.

Despite the unorthodox welcome, the trail breakers used their machines to pack a takeoff track for Sammy's Cub. He flew out just before darkness fell. There was nothing to do for Danny's heavier plane except let nature take its course and freeze the sugary snow into a runway. Danny could wait overnight with his plane, or head on with the trail breakers to Ruby. Assured by his trail-breaking friends that Ruby couldn't be more than a few hours away, Danny decided a cozy place to bunk for the night was a better option than staying with the plane. He piled onto one of the machines and the group headed toward Ruby.

Danny spent most of the next 15 hours struggling, along with his chuckling, snowmachine-driving friends, to dig out, or push, or pull, or pry the sluggish machines through the heavy drifts that bogged them down the entire 75 miles to Ruby. Worse conditions along the way have been rare. Paybacks are never long in coming on the trail.

17 Shaktoolik

Not until the arctic coast is reached at Unalakleet and the race turns north does the event begin to feel like it's entering the home stretch. But the race is still far from over at this point. Up ahead, first of all, is the long string of coastal houses that constitute Shaktoolik. It's a desolate place. Veterinarian Sonny King told me that he "spent three days there last Thursday." Another vet told me that in the dictionary, "under the definition of desolate, the only word is Shaktoolik."

On a crystal-clear day in Shaktoolik, mist can be seen rising from the open water off shore. Closer in, bright sunshine and an open lead of water through the ice will have seals basking along the edges as if they were sprawling on the white sand of a Florida beach. They may appear lethargic but are not. At the slightest provocation, they plunge back into the frigid water.

As in all coastal villages, fishing is pretty much the main occupation. Boats and skiffs stick out of nearly every snowbank. The village once moved inland along the sloping hills to what seemed an idyllic setting. Wood was more readily available to warm the little houses when the cold bit deeply in the darkness of winter, and there was protection from the unrelenting coastal wind. But it didn't work. In the non-snowy portion of the arctic year, mosquitoes rule what the ocean does not. Mosquitoes swarm so thickly that getting a breath of clean air without choking on the bugs is more of a concern than the bites they inflict. Wind is your friend if mosquitoes are your enemy. The people in Shaktoolik are content with the wind.

Pilots landing at Shaktoolik have several options, not all of them attractive. Planes without skis can land on the wind-blown dirt runway. Planes with skis can try the somewhat protected frozen slough behind the village, though wind is always a problem. Or they can try to find room out front on the ocean ice, between the uplifted chunks and frozen drifts. And almost always, blowing snow is there to do you in if you make a mistake.

The excitement of the Iditarod draws many volunteer pilots into the affair. But the wind and the cold and the tough conditions of a place like Shaktoolik soon weed out the pilots without genuine enthusiasm for being part of the race.

DON BOWERS IS A PILOT with the spirit and enthusiasm of a born Iditarod flyer. As a colonel in the "real" air force, he flew a four-engine C-130. He juggled his time so he could help with the race, flying his own Cessna 206, on wheels.

His retirement after twenty-four years in the U.S. Air Force has given him even more time to devote to his Iditarod passion. Like several other Iditarod Air Force pilots before him, Bowers finally put together his own dog team and ran the race as a musher. He made it to Nome on the back of a sled in 1996, experiencing in person much of what he had seen from the air as a pilot.

In his journal of the 1991 race, Bowers tells a remarkable tale of what it takes to be a dedicated Iditarod pilot. The story starts in Unalakleet, but all the drama takes place in Shaktoolik.

Following is an edited excerpt from the journal:

AFTER A LONG DAY OF FLYING that started in McGrath ten hours earlier, I land at Unalakleet and start to put the airplane away. But Pat Plunkett, the logistics coordinator, tells me she has another mission. Tony Turinsky has gotten tied up at White Mountain and can't get into Shaktoolik to pick up eleven dropped dogs, including one that's in serious shape with a ruptured eye.

The weather looks like it'll hold awhile, so I find my helper from New Zealand, Snow Holwill, and we fly north along the coastal trail. I call Nome Flight Service to get some weather for Shaktoolik, but they don't have any reports from there. All they can tell me is that it looks good at Unalakleet and there's nothing serious forecast for the next few hours.

As we leave the hills to go out the spit toward Shaktoolik, I look for the village. Normally I can see it easily from the hills, but I now see only an indistinct haze. I also notice the outside air temperature on the airplane thermometer is dropping rapidly from the balmy 10-above we've enjoyed since leaving Unalakleet.

As we descend and head farther out the peninsula, the wind starts to kick up on the ground, blowing from the north-northeast. The temperature continues to drop sharply. I call it out to Snow as it drops through minus 10, minus 15, minus 18, minus 19—all in the space of a couple of minutes. Running at 300 feet along the beach, I can see the wind is kicking up the snow to make a ground blizzard, reducing ground visibility to a mile or less while leaving the in-flight visibility undisturbed a hundred feet overhead.

The wind steadily increases as we get closer to the ground and farther out from the hills. I'm carrying almost a 30-degree "crab"—turned partially into the wind—in order to stay parallel to the beach and the trail. I think I see Shaktoolik a couple of times, but it's only the reduced visibility playing tricks on me. Finally we see the village, and I figure I can handle what I estimate to be 20- or 25-knot winds.

I find the approach end of the runway without much difficulty; the far end is obscured in the ground blizzard, but I expected that. I drop the flaps and touch down without much trouble, but as I'm trying to slow down we keep getting gusts that try to float the airplane. I'm on the ground taxiing at a slow walk, trying to find someplace to turn around, when the airplane comes to a mushy stop in a nearly invisible 2-foot-deep snowdrift that blocks the runway. I try to power through it, and a ferocious gust hits the airplane and lifts the right wing up almost to a 40-degree angle; the left wingtip is within a foot of the ground for a couple of seconds before the plane settles back to an even keel.

At that point I decide I've underestimated the wind and everything else and that I've let myself get suckered into a very serious situation. It's time to get out any way we can. The wind is now blowing at least 40 knots (I learn later that it was even worse than that: 50 knots, gusting to 70), and the temperature is somewhere below minus 20. The plane is stuck in a crusted snowdrift over the tops of the tires. We can't leave the plane here because there's no way to tie it down, and another gust like the one we just went through will flip it.

I absolutely must try to take off again, and quickly. The first order of business is to move enough snow from around the wheels to allow the plane to go forward. I don't have time to pull on my cold-weather gear, so I jump out of the airplane without gloves or hat and instantly frostbite the tips of at least three fingers as well as every square inch of exposed skin. In all my years in Alaska, I've never felt cold bite as hard as this.

I kick snow from in front of the wheels, then lean almost double into the wind to walk down the runway to see if there are any snowdrifts that will block a takeoff. Sure enough, there's one about 200 feet down, but the plane should clear it easily with this headwind.

Back in the plane, I drop half-flaps for a max-effort takeoff, tell Snow to hold on, and pour on the coal. Now I'm hoping for a big gust to give us instant lift out of the snowdrift. After a couple of seconds the plane slowly moves forward; we get a solid gust that gives enough oomph to clear the drift. Almost immediately I get flying speed and hold on for all I'm worth to stay airborne. We're helped by the fact that the super-cold air is probably causing the engine to crank out 50 extra horsepower.

As soon as we break ground, we're in a complete white-out, but this is something I can handle, thanks to twenty years of U.S. Air Force instrument training and the extra bucks I've spent on keeping the airplane up to standards. We pop out over the top of the blowing snow in another few seconds, circle back over the town, and head for Unalakleet at warp speed.

Snow doesn't say much through all of this, but about halfway back we decide it's Miller time as soon as we land. Unalakleet is a "personal consumption only" town and there's nothing alcoholic for sale, but Snow has some Canadian Hunter in his pack, so we decide that'll do. I call Nome radio and tell them in no uncertain terms the runway at Shaktoolik is closed.

18 Unalakleet

Don Bowers has seen some of the best and the worst that the Iditarod can throw at a volunteer pilot. Here, in this edited excerpt from his 1991 Iditarod journal, Bowers gives us a close look at the end of a very tough day in Unalakleet:

A FEW MILES FROM UNALAKLEET, it's obvious the weather is going down, and very quickly. The wind has shifted to blow from the east and is up to 20 or 30 knots; the ceiling is down to less than a thousand feet and the visibility is less than a mile in snow and blowing snow. I land into the gale on runway 08, and Snow and I tie the airplane down in a hurry.

A group of us load into the pickup and head downtown to the Stanton Oyoumick Gymnasium. It's not exactly the Sheraton, but it'll do. The pilots and other race people are sleeping in a big room at the southwest end of the building.

Downstairs is a makeshift kitchen stocked with trail food. We're all starved, and Dorothea Taylor makes some macaroni and hamburger. Somebody produces a box of banana creme ice cream, which is gone in a couple of minutes; we assume the trail committee decided to leave us a treat. We were wrong. The ice cream turns out to belong to one of the ham radio operators, who bought western Alaska's last carton of that flavor that afternoon at the local Northern Commercial general store. He practically has a stroke when he finds the empty box later in the evening.

I walk out to the airport about ten that evening to check the airplane. The wind is howling out of the east at 30 knots; the temperature is zero and dropping. I'm wearing everything in my survival bag, including long johns, heavy shirt, quilted jacket, heavy parka, thick gloves, wool muffler, fur-lined pilot's hat, and I have the parka hood up—and the cold still comes right through.

It's about a mile out to the airport. The main street is a snow canyon lined with 8- to 10-foot drifts that have been chewed out by the highway department with a big snow blower. There are side canyons cut for streets and driveways. The only traffic is a few snowmachines and all-terrain vehicles, driven by bundled-up figures who can't possibly see where they're going. I keep well to the side of the street until I'm safely at the edge of town.

As I get toward the airport, the road runs along the beach, totally exposed; there's no place to hide. I half-feel my way into the airport parking area, and over the wind I can hear wing covers flapping madly. Mine are OK, and the tie-downs are holding. Wing covers on two of the other planes are almost in shreds, and I tighten them down as best I can. I've got an electric heater tucked up inside my engine cowling, but the wind is sucking the heat out as fast as it's being generated.

I hide in the shelter of one of the hangars until I'm ready to face the return walk to town. On the way back, I stop for a few minutes on the beach road, looking out into the darkness over Norton Sound; the next stop is Siberia, only a couple of hundred miles to the west. For the first time, I really notice the howl of the wind, a sort of low, wavering, primeval moan, straight from the heart of the last ice age. I suddenly feel intensely, inexplicably lonely. Imagine being totally alone on the tundra, unable to escape that unending wail. I hustle back through the snow canyons as fast as I can.

BACK AT THE GYM, the radio operator tells me that checkpoints on up the coast are reporting hurricane-force winds with chill factors well below minus 100. No wonder Snow and I had had such a terrifying time of it when we landed earlier that day at Shaktoolik. With the weather getting bad even by Bering Sea standards, everyone is trying to figure out the location of the dog teams that are still on the trail.

Kazuo Kojima, whom we saw that afternoon before the storm hit, is the next one expected in from Kaltag. His flashlight is seen bobbing for what seems like an hour through the blowing snow as he slowly makes his way across the frozen lagoon that borders Unalakleet on the east. He finally shows up 20 minutes before midnight, having taken more than eight hours to cover the last 10 miles in the blizzard.

In the midst of the screaming wind and horizontal snow, first things must come first: the checker counts the dogs, inventories the sled, and formally notes Kojima's arrival time at the checkpoint. All is in order, except that Kojima's high-tech Japanese headlight isn't working. New lithium batteries supposedly are being flown in, if anyone can get through this storm.

Rich Hardin speaks a few words of Japanese to him, and Kojima seems very pleased that anyone is making an attempt to be courteous in such a bleak place. The race judge tells him he shouldn't try to go any farther tonight because of the abominable conditions ahead; in fact, they're discouraging any musher from leaving the checkpoints from Kaltag to Elim until things get better. I help lead Kojima's dogs the quarter-mile up to the gymnasium. His whole team seems to be in surprisingly good shape, considering the storm they've just come through, and they literally drag me and the other volunteer handlers up the road.

Before we can get Kojima squared away, a totally blitzed Native staggers up and insists that Kojima stay at his house tonight. Kojima is a dignified, gray-haired Japanese gentleman, and he's profoundly embarrassed; he doesn't speak much English and not a word of Yup'ik, and he doesn't know what to do. All of us, including the checker, stand around nervously, hoping the would-be host will wander off home before anything untoward happens. In a few minutes, a village public safety officer arrives and takes

the well-meaning celebrant in tow for overnight obser-
vation.

After Kojima's dogs are fed and bedded down, we have
hot chocolate ready for him inside, and he appears most
grateful. Although we can't communicate too well, he
seems to be a fine person, the sort of well-to-do adventurer
that Alaska has attracted for years. I don't know any
rational reason for his running the race, but then I can't
imagine why anyone would be trying to fly planes here,
either.

19   Ace Dodson

March 15, 1980, *Anchorage Daily News:* "Spaniards, Pilot Die in Crash."

Like many others who fly during the race, Ace Dodson was not part of the volunteer Iditarod Air Force. But when you pilot an airplane, the risks are equal for all. Warren (Ace) Dodson and the three Spaniards he was carrying aboard his airplane all died when the plane plummeted into the sea ice just south of Shaktoolik. It's the worst disaster that has occurred during the race.

Ace was a pilot for Wien airlines, but during the Iditarod, he usually took work on his own, flying his vintage 1936 Gullwing Stinson, the one he called *Bird*. This year, however, he had leased a Cessna 185, equipped with wheel skis, to accommodate a Spanish film crew and their equipment. They were shooting a documentary.

All the way up the trail, the Spaniards won the hearts of everyone they encountered. Music filled every checkpoint they visited for the night as they sang and played guitar. Ace had established his partying reputation along the trail years ago and was well-known and liked. Ace and the Spaniards were well-matched as they laughed and sang their way toward Nome.

DICK MACKEY AND HIS WIFE, KATHY, were reluctant witnesses to disaster. Dick was competing in the race but had to scratch in Unalakleet when he became ill. Kathy flew up to Unalakleet to pick him up in their Cessna 180 and fly him to Nome for medical treatment. Two others also boarded the plane for the flight to Nome: pilot Anna Lampley, and Verona Thompson, another musher who had to quit the race. By chance, the plane piloted by Kathy fell in with a flight of two other airplanes. One was piloted by Tony Oney Sr. The other carried Ace Dodson and the Spaniards.

Kathy's plane was behind and slightly above Dodson's as they flew up the coast toward Shaktoolik. Tony's plane developed radio trouble almost immediately. Dick, serving as radio operator for the flight, heard Tony's announcement to Dodson that he was turning back, and he watched as Tony peeled off from Dodson's left and disappeared behind them. When the radio crackled again, the voice was Dodson's—just a quick exclamation that made it clear he was in trouble.

In horror, the Mackeys and their passengers watched as the plane in front of them slammed into the ice and snow below, disintegrating before their eyes. Dick was on the radio immediately with a Mayday call.

In the excitement, the message was misunderstood, and the FAA thought it was Mackey who was in trouble. Kathy found a clear spot on the ice near the wreck and landed. Other planes soon arrived as well.

One of Dick's acquaintances walked up to him. "We heard it was you, Dick!"

MIKE AND DEE BARBARICK, serving as ham radio operators for the race, had become quite close to the Spaniards. Mike spoke a little Spanish and was one of the few people who could communicate directly with them. He once helped them repair some film equipment they desperately needed, using a soldering iron he kept with his radio supplies. And if that wasn't enough to cement their relationship, the partying and singing they all enjoyed at night did. A close friendship developed as they all moved up the trail together.

It was Dee who first picked up the Morse code message as it was being transmitted down the line to headquarters. Normally the hams used voice communication, but they wanted to keep the accident a bit quiet until the families of the victims could be notified. Dee couldn't believe what she was hearing, and asked Mike to listen as well.

"Dodson . . . probably killed . . . the whole Spanish film crew . . ." Mike and Dee were speechless.

The Spaniards had left just the day before from a checkpoint where Mike and Dee were stationed. Mike shot some 8-millimeter footage of their takeoff as a commemorative of the good times they had together.

Mike helped the National Transportation Safety Board piece together the cause of the accident. It was a disaster waiting to happen. The Canadian aviation authorities had actually already figured out the problem behind this kind of accident. It was associated with the center line on Cessna 185s and the way in which skis were attached. The Canadians were now attaching the spring-loaded front ski-lifting cables out to the sides of the engine cowling instead of to the landing-gear attachment points, as was the practice in this country at the time of Ace Dodson's crash.

Cases had been documented in Canada in which the speed of the aircraft caused enough wind pressure on the landing-gear mounts to rotate the skis over center and into a straight-down configuration–creating, in effect, instant air brakes. The Canadians widened the distance between the mounts by putting the attachment points farther out on the plane, and that seemed to solve the problem. Today it is the only way skis are attached to 185s in both countries.

20 End of a Career

How a pilot reacts to an "incident" is often an indication of his experience level. What may have almost caused a pilot heart failure at one time may not even be worth mentioning at a later stage of his flying career. "Fender benders" in the bush can be a hardship, but they seem to be an accepted part of life. The inconvenience of having one's bird out of commission for repairs is usually taken in stride.

Pilots have a curious tendency to understate the seriousness of these mishaps. Perhaps no one exemplifies that tendency more than the Father of the Iditarod Air Force himself. Larry Thompson gave a lot more to the Iditarod than 10 years of his life. At a time when insurance was an unthinkable expenditure for the Iditarod budget, Larry donated more than his time to the cause. He speaks casually of the Iditarod incidents that beat up two of his planes.

During work on one race, Larry caught a ski in a snow berm at Finger Lake and cartwheeled his 180. He walked away without a scratch, but the plane wasn't so lucky.

"It was rebuildable though," he quickly added, as if that one didn't count.

Of course the plane was uninsured—quite a gift from a working man toward an event that now operates with a budget in seven figures and pays the winner as much as 50 grand!

It was not the only airplane Larry rebuilt, thanks to the Iditarod. A Cessna 185 that he was leasing for his air taxi business ended up in a heap as well. Larry was not at the controls, though. He was busy trying to work his rebuilt 180 on skis out of McGrath during one of those years when snow in the Interior was slim to nonexistent.

Since the 185 was fitted with wheel skis, and since there was plenty of snow back home in Anchorage, Larry decided to switch the airplanes. He hired a fellow to fly the wheel-ski plane to McGrath.

"The guy claimed he had tons of flight time, and Alaskan experience to boot," Larry told me with a mischievous grin.

"Well," he continued, shaking his head, "the fellow wound up missing Rainy Pass, but not the mountains."

Lost for nearly a week, the pilot hired by Larry was eventually found, unhurt. Larry never worried about the damaged plane because it was fully insured. However, the accident investigation ferreted out some discrepancies in the pilot's flight-time requirements, and the insurance company refused to pay for the damages.

"So I got to pay for that one, too," Larry said. Another gift to the cause.

AN EXPERIENCE IN NOME, while not costing Larry any money, marked an end to his contributions of aircraft. The race was winding down and everyone was starting to think about the trip home. Larry's 180 was parked on the sea ice in front of the convention center.

Larry thought he had seen it all during his 10 years with the Iditarod, but nothing prepared him for the fellow who ran up to him, yelling, "Hey, Larry, your airplane is sinking!"

Sure enough, when he got to the plane, water was already up over the wheel skis. A little higher, and he would be looking at another rebuild, this time due to salt-water corrosion. But the plane wasn't sinking. The tide had come flooding in over the shore ice instead of flowing beneath the ice, as it usually did. Luckily, tidal changes in Norton Sound are minimal. The water never came up high enough to cause serious damage.

But when the water finally retreated, Larry was ready to do the same. The end of an era had arrived.

"Ten years is enough!" he announced.

21 Anvik and the Yukon

The hillside Athabaskan settlement of Anvik is one of the most picturesque villages along the trail. Its cozy log cabins are snuggled in among the spruce and birch above the mighty Yukon that winds through the valley. It's easy to see why the cabins are situated so far up the hillside when you walk up from the ice of the slough that angles off the river and pass a high-water marker tacked to the power pole by the town's only store and lodge. By standing in just the right place on the upward-sloping snow-packed trail beside the pole, you can position your eye level exactly even with the sign and look out over the broad expanse of the valley to the east. Little more than swamps with patches of brush, and some higher ground with stunted black spruce and scattered hardwoods, stretch out to the distant hills nearly 18 trail miles away.

How much water would it take to fill the valley to put the sign where it is? The question is futile, for the answer is almost beyond imagining. I decide that whoever thought

114

up the term "mighty" to describe the Yukon was a master of understatement. But every word I try as a replacement pales before the immense volume of water I picture before me. I make a mental note to fly out here someday when the river is at its highest, during the spring ice breakup. I'm glad the town's highest point is the airport.

Anvik is along the southern route for the Iditarod, the trail variation that the race takes on odd-numbered years. When the race reaches the relative safety of the Yukon at Anvik, the trail turns directly up the Yukon for the next 150 or so miles to Kaltag.

It's a welcome change for pilots and mushers alike to travel a route where it's hard to get lost, since they simply have to follow the big river. This is the only section of the race where pilots get the opportunity for true IFR flying. IFR may officially mean Instrument Flight Rules, but to pilots who fly in the bush, it really means "I follow rivers; I follow roads; I follow railroads."

The first musher to reach the river at Anvik is welcomed by the ringing of the church bell and the famous seven-course dinner rumored to cost in the neighborhood of five thousand dollars. Of course, volunteer pilots will already have been in and out of the village countless times in the days and weeks before the bell rings. And if they're lucky, they will have received a prepared meal of hot soup and crackers.

PAT VARNEY FLEW INTO ANVIK during the 1987 Iditarod with race marshal Bobby Lee. Pat was hauling Bobby along

115

the trail that year, and Bobby wanted to make sure all was ready at Anvik for the arrival of the first mushers. Not lucky enough for soup and crackers, Pat and Bobby grabbed a PB&J sandwich (lifeblood of volunteers along the trail) before climbing back into the 170 to head farther north.

Pat taxied to the far end of the little winding slough just off the main river upstream of the village. A hard wind blew in off the river. The 170 accelerated down the slough and started leftward around the first bend, but the skis wanted to slide sideways to the right. The rudder and the torque of the engine were trying to drag the skis around the bend, to the left and into the wind. But it wasn't enough. The right wing caught the brush along the bank and pulled the airplane around. The left ski dug in and collapsed. The left wing followed suit.

The airplane tumbled up and over itself, snow flying everywhere as it landed on its roof. Skidding upside-down across a frozen gravel bar, it tumbled a second time before stopping abruptly in a huge snowdrift.

Loose powdery snow filtered into every unfilled space within the plane. Bobby kicked open a door and dragged Pat out with him. Neither man was hurt—but when they looked at the pile of crinkled aluminum and broken parts and shattered Plexiglas, they wondered how they had escaped unscathed.

The last anyone saw of the crumpled bird was when it went around the bend on its way downriver to Holy Cross, trussed up and tied to a sledge behind a snowmachine. There it would get loaded aboard a Northern Air Cargo

DC-6 for the flight to Anchorage, where a total rebuild was in order. While the first musher into Anvik was washing down the last of his seven-course dinner with fine wine, Pat was swallowing the last of a beer. Then he could worry about how to pay for the airplane.

22 Rescuing the Colonel

To remain in the headlines with the Iditarod, you have to be a good promoter. To work unselfishly in the background, often risking more than you can afford to lose, you only have to be a volunteer pilot.

Mike Moore, of Kodiak, is just such a person. He started flying the trail under Larry Thompson back in 1978 and finally took over as chief pilot around 1983 when Larry bowed out.

During six of the years Mike flew the trail, he took a month off from his lineman job, without pay, to help with the race. His Piper PA-12 was modified considerably over the years: 160-horsepower engine, Borer prop, Super Cub tail feathers and flaps. The plane was a real performer, and Mike utilized it to its full potential.

"I like it because it's big and roomy," he says. Mike needs the room. Big, burly, and bearded, Mike has made more than his share of contributions to the race. In 1982 alone, he flew 78 hours just hauling the race marshal around. During his time as chief pilot, the race dominated a huge part of his year.

"The month that the race is on isn't the only time you are busy," he says. For instance, "someone has to see to it that the gas cache for Unalakleet gets on the fuel barge, which only operates in the summer."

Mike came naturally to bush flying. His folks homesteaded forty acres after they arrived in Alaska in 1946, and his mom used to take him to the school bus stop by dog sled. His dad, "Moose" Moore, was a flight instructor at Merrill Field in Anchorage when Mike was growing up. Eventually the whole family became involved with a project of the state's fish and game department to relocate animals out into the wilds. Like so many others who grew up in the bush, Mike found flying to be as natural as driving on freeways is for other people.

This easiness about bush flying came through loud and clear in an interview with Mike in *Alaska Flying* magazine. It seems that Mike was summoned to go pick up Iditarod official Rosemary Phillips, who had gotten soaked when the snowmachine she was riding hit some overflow water on the ice of the Little Susitna River, on the Anchorage side of the race. Hypothermia set in even though her companions had wrapped Rosemary in sleeping bags. It was obvious she was in extreme danger unless she could be flown out.

Here's what Mike told the magazine reporter:

"I went in and landed in a swampy area filled with brush. I got her into the plane but barely cleared the trees on the takeoff. At Lake Hood the ambulance was there to meet us."

I couldn't get much more from Mike than the reporter had. But you can be sure Rosemary's rescue wasn't quite that easy.

MIKE WAS JUST AS MATTER-OF-FACT in describing his adventure with Colonel Norman Vaughan, who was in his seventies at the time. The colonel, good promoter that he is, was still finding backers to send him up the trail as a musher. His brain may still have been as sharp as that of a 25-year-old, but his body was not.

With his sled smashed and his ankle sprained in a freak accident somewhere along the Farewell Burn area between Rohn and Nikolai, race officials considered sending a helicopter out to rescue the colonel, but Mike went instead in his PA-12.

Mike didn't go out of cockiness—entirely. But when you have finished first at the Gulkana Air Show in the short-field landings division and have heard the announcer introduce you by saying "Here comes Mike's helicopter," it would be easy to get that way.

Here's all that Mike said for the magazine about the incident:

"I flew out the trail from McGrath, spotted him, and found a tiny spot to land. In fact, when the plane stopped, I had only about 10 feet of space to spare. I got him and his gear aboard and flew him back to McGrath for medical attention."

That's a pretty terse statement; certainly not the version

that would come from someone who was seeking headlines. What really happened is this:

Race marshal Jim Kershner asked Mike to fly him out to the area to see what was happening. Kershner, who is every bit as big as Mike, climbed into the PA-12 with Mike, and they flew out along the trail until they spotted the colonel.

Kershner hadn't intended to do much more than look the situation over from the air. He knew the Farewell Burn doesn't usually provide safe landing areas. But Mike saw a spot he thought he could manage, and he took the plane down. There actually was only feet to spare as he brought the bird to a halt.

Kershner realized that Vaughan could not go on. Regardless of what the colonel's 25-year-old mind might have been telling him, his body was reporting something far different.

They all waited until a fellow on a snowmachine, summoned from Nikolai, arrived to take care of the dogs and the broken sled. Then Vaughan and some of his gear were loaded into the plane, and Kershner and Mike climbed back in.

Kershner said that Mike's handling of the flight out of the Burn was the best piece of flying he'd ever seen. Coming from a pilot who has handled just about every position associated with the Iditarod, that's quite a testimonial.

Getting the plane off the jumbled ground of the Burn and over the brush was only part of the challenge. There was a ridge to clear as well. Mike was cool and calculated the whole time. He knew the risks—but he also knew what he and his airplane could do.

Vaughan continued to enter the Iditarod after that. He finished sixtieth among sixty-one finishers in the 1990 race, when he was in his eighties. It's hard to know what would have happened if Mike had not had the skill to bring his little plane in and out of the rescue site safely. But it's certain he would still be paying for the privilege of rescuing the colonel.

23　Rookie at Rohn

For the pilots who fly the trail, the airstrip at the Rohn checkpoint might just as well be labeled "Caution" on the charts. It can be one of the true pilot challenges along the route. You can't depend on the surface: one time it's ice, another time deep snow, then half snow and half wind-blown gravel. But you can depend on the wind: there's almost always a difficult crosswind.

At this airstrip, you usually have two choices for landing or takeoff. First, uphill toward the trees, with a quartering headwind—a situation that has you wondering whether you will slide to a stop before the trees get you on landing or be able to clear them on takeoff. And second, downhill, with no barriers in the way. Your only worry then is the quartering tailwind and the question of whether you will be down and stopped on landing or solidly in the air on takeoff before falling off the unobstructed bank and into the partially frozen Kuskokwim River.

These were the choices that Fred Herman mulled over

before flying out with eight dogs aboard his Cessna 180. He decided to take off uphill, but didn't quite clear the trees. By the time the snow and dirt and tree branches and flying debris had settled, eight dogs had made tracks into the bush. The 180 had to stay behind until new wings arrived. Later that spring, some of the air force pilots returned on their own to cut back the trees, lengthening the runway.

The picturesque little cabin at Rohn, nestled among a thick stand of white spruce beside the runway, is a welcome sight to all who come there. Used by countless travelers, prospectors, and trappers over the years, the cabin has always remained in serviceable condition. The building is one of the countless structures known as roadhouses that still dot the sectional charts of the state, though most have long ago sunk into the moss underfoot. The full official name of Rohn is, in fact, Rohn Roadhouse.

Who knows how many times the cabin has been rebuilt, reroofed, or repaired over the years? It has always been stocked with emergency firewood and a supply of food, and there never was a lock on the door. And all without handouts from any government agency. Whoever seemed to need it most at the time saw to it that repairs were made. Trapper Scotty Mileur was the last to use the cabin on a regular basis before the federal government, in the form of the Bureau of Land Management, officially laid claim to it and said it was off-limits to other users. Scotty was ousted. And now, even the Iditarod has to have a permit to use the cabin. So much for progress.

PILOT DAVE FETZNER also faced the decision on how to depart Rohn as he got ready to fly out with nine dogs during the 1994 race. He decided to take off downhill. It was another decision that caused the trouble.

First you need to know a little about Dave. One look at his immaculate logbooks and other paperwork and you know he is some sort of engineer, a man who likes to keep things in perfect order. It only follows that his airplane would have barely a mark on it, inside or out.

This was only his second trip into Rohn. The first was just a day or so earlier, in crosswinds that white-knuckled him so much that his German passenger commented, "It vas a goot landing but you sure vas vite!"

Dave had never hauled dogs before. He knew that dogs pee, and often don't care where. To prevent getting his airplane soiled inside, he removed the back seats and carefully hung a plastic tarp around the interior, creating a loose, pee-tight container. The only small detail that wasn't solved was what to tie the dogs to, as all the attachment points were now covered by the tarp. He decided to deal with that issue on a later flight. For now, he would leave the dogs loose in the plane. At least they wouldn't mess it up.

The dogs were piled in, and Dave fired up the engine. He wasn't alone at the airstrip. Some of the other air force members were there, and a video camera was rolling. The story had spread of Dave's white-knuckled introduction to Rohn, and his fellow pilots were not about to miss another opportunity to see how the Rohn rookie performed. He had nailed his second landing just fine; they would now see what he would do with dogs on the departure.

No sooner had Dave started his takeoff run downhill toward the open river than he realized he had some amorous souls on board. True to form, the female dog was playing hard to get. The 185's torque was trying to turn the plane to the left. Dave was hard on the right rudder and in total concentration while easing back on the yoke for liftoff. It was then the female leaped over the back of the front seat and practically into his lap, with the males about to follow. Almost without thinking, Dave slammed the reluctant female back into her tongue-panting suitors just as the 185 lifted off.

The commotion started again. Still shaking from the takeoff, Dave did not hesitate. He sent the plane into a quick drop several times, giving the dogs a few rather violent "space flights," trying to shock them into behaving. The female apparently changed her mind at some point, and then all Dave could hear was the rapid thump, thump, thumping of the loose tarp in the back. At least one of his passengers was satisfied with the way things had worked out.

The video that had been shot by Dave's flying buddies was shown to a packed house that night in a big room above Rosa's cafe in McGrath. Dave was the guest of honor. Glaringly absent as part of the film was Dave's fine landing the second time he set down at Rohn. Instead, all the audience saw was the dog-laden takeoff.

They saw the 185 start down the runway, weaving back and forth. Not pictured, of course, was the drama inside the plane, as Dave fought the rudder to maintain control. At liftoff, things got worse. The right wingtip nearly touched

126

the runway as the left one raised skyward. The horizontal stabilizer, with the quartering tailwind, stayed as danger-ously low as the nose was high while the whole bird slid to the right, nearly clipping the trees on the side of the strip closest to the cabin. Dave took a lot of ribbing. But later, at McGuires tavern, he was toasted time and again. The rookie at Rohn had graduated.

The next morning, Dave cut holes in the bottom of the "pee bag" to get at the tie-downs, so he could secure the next load of dogs. Having an immaculate airplane is nice, but keeping it in one piece is even better.

24 Buffalo Country

Getting through Rainy Pass and into the Interior is a milestone whether you're on the back runners of a sled or the front seat of a Super Cub. Once a pilot leaves Puntilla Lake and heads toward the mountains, even with the weather bright and sunny, the actual entrance to the pass is not easy to spot. Several openings into the hills beckon. It is the wise aviator who, in good visibility, makes some close observations of the ground in the event that marginal weather fills the valley, as it often does. The small lake just at the entrance to the pass is a good checkpoint.

And now the pass. Veer to the right and start climbing. You may see caribou on the hillsides. Almost always there are tracks. The sun can be glorious in here, below the peaks. By climbing through at minimal altitude, you get a good look at how the actual trail runs beneath you on the ground. Every detail is important. Another turn to the left as you gain the downhill side of the pass. Ease back on the power. Kind of narrow at this low altitude, but safe enough

128

in a Super Cub. Out onto the drainages that lead to Dalzell Creek, then another turn to the right. Tatina River is dead ahead, as is the famous Dalzell Gorge where dogs and mushers make their way down the icy slopes to the waiting river below.

Scotty Mileur, who has done plenty of guiding and trapping in these parts, says the gorge was not always the real trail.

"No miner in his right mind would risk losing everything he had just to make up some time. In the old days, they had cut a trail through the sidehill alders."

And sure enough, there's the old trail on the left as we come out onto the river—easily spotted from this bird's-eye view even though grown up with brush. There is good reason why no one has taken the time in our modern days of snowmachine travel and speed to keep the old trail open. Avalanches! They can sweep down from the mountaintops at any time.

More than once, an F-15 fighter from nearby Elmendorf Air Force Base, loaded with enough firepower to start and finish World War III, has slipped away from war games to scream its way through the pass at low altitude in order to dislodge snow prior to race time. A discreet telephone call or an after-hours get-together with a few sympathetic U.S. Air Force guys can get amazing things accomplished. Whether the Pentagon is aware of such goings-on is not known.

Turning left, it is now only a short hop down the Tatina River to Rohn. The passage through Rainy Pass and on to Rohn is a multifaceted transition. Not only have you crossed the Alaska Range and officially entered the Interior, but you have come into an entirely new weather system as well. For the mushers, it is here the trail changes dramatically. The rough section known as the Farewell Burn is up ahead, and so are the buffalo.

A HERD OF AMERICAN BUFFALO (or bison) was introduced from Montana to the Delta area, southeast of Fairbanks, in the 1940s, and some of the animals were transplanted to the area near Rohn in the 1960s. From the original thirty-eight animals, the Rohn herd numbers around 300 today. The herd size is kept in check through a drawing system that provides about fifty hunting permits a year.

It's a treat to see these great animals in an area where you expect to spot only moose or caribou. Mushers tell some good tales of their encounters with the critters along the trail, but from a grandstand seat with wings, just looking isn't bad.

Floyd Tetpon spotted several of the buffalo on a tiny lake one day, and he circled a couple of times before continuing on to McGrath. The race marshal was with him, and both men were commenting on the magnificence of the animals when something apparently broke loose in the engine of the Super Cub.

"It was really making a clatter," Floyd said when I talked to him that afternoon.

"Son of a bitch!" is what the race marshal heard at the time.

Floyd cut the fuel supply to the engine and headed for the lake while he called the FAA people at McGrath radio. They got a fix on him just as he was dead-sticking a landing onto the trackless white that stretched in all directions.

Floyd opened the engine cowling and found nothing. Walking around to open the other side, he discovered it wasn't the engine that was making the noise after all. The left wing-root faring had come loose on the top and had been trying to beat the side of his fabric-covered airplane into pulp. With a pocket knife, Floyd cut off the dangling piece of aluminum, and they were soon under way once again. Another normal flying day in buffalo country.

"Kind of put my heart in my throat for a while, though," Floyd admitted.

25 Iditarod Hot Dogs

You Drop Em, We Chop Em" read the sign over the Iditadog Cafe that welcomed everyone to the gold-mining ghost town of Iditarod, halfway point of the 1993 race. This new feature had been added along the route without knowledge of the Iditarod Trail Committee, and the powers-that-be were not taking it well. This kind of thing was not in keeping with the image the committee tried to present to the world. Nearly everyone went into hysterics when it dawned on them what the sign was talking about. Specialty of the house? Hot dogs! What else?

ABC took full advantage of the novelty and conducted many of its halfway-point interviews from the balcony of the hastily erected cafe. Back in the early 1900s, the Iditadog Cafe would not have raised an eyebrow among the thousands of gold-seekers who swarmed into the area of Iditarod (an Indian word variously translated as "clear water" or "distant place"). The dilapidated cabins of the brothels that came with the onslaught are still recognizable behind the cafe, as are the abandoned bank and general store across the Iditarod River.

Fully intended to be the prank that it was, the Iditadog Cafe was not the brainchild of the Iditarod Air Force, though you might have thought so. The whole thing was dreamed up by Mark and Sherri Kepler and Tad Fullerton, who all live in Flat, just over the hill from Iditarod.

"We decided the Iditarod was getting too serious about itself and decided to lighten things up a bit," Mark told me over a deliciously warmed-up and gooey cinnamon roll and hot coffee the first morning the cafe was open.

The Keplers and Fullerton are only three of a handful of people who still call Flat home. There is a gravel runway there, and a smattering of cabins. In the old days, supplies and gold-mining equipment were hauled from Iditarod to Flat over a log trail after being delivered to Iditarod by the shallow-draft steamboats that plied the river. Iditarod was the nearest "big city" to Flat.

I'D BEEN TO FLAT ONLY ONCE when race manager Jack Niggemyer asked me if I would fly "Freight Train" from McGrath back to his cabin in Flat. Jack was paying back a favor to one of the least likely of Iditarod Trail benefactors. Freight Train, as you might imagine, filled the back seat of the Super Cub. I never did learn his actual name. The scars on his face and his reputation for drinking whiskey by the water-glass full don't tell you much about the real man. When he climbed into my Cub in 10-below weather wearing a T-shirt and bib overalls, casually tossing his jacket into the back, I figured that not all the stories about him were unfounded. Freight Train claimed he owned the cabin that served as the race checkpoint at Iditarod. And even if he didn't, who was going to argue with him?

What the scars and the reputation don't even hint at is his vast knowledge of the area—an area so remote and desolate, you wonder why anyone would even be here. Freight Train had trapped in the area, and he knew practically every ravine we crossed. In fact, I couldn't have asked for a more knowledgeable or congenial passenger.

The reasons that hold people such as Freight Train in a wild country like this are as much a mystery as what really lured them to the area nearly a century ago. Perhaps it was simply the gold. Or was Robert Service right: "It's not the gold they're wantin' but the search."

Maybe it was the vastness of the land. Or the sound of a wolf howling on a distant hillside. Or that special blood that runs in the veins of some people and lets them do what the rest of us only wonder about. I wondered plenty about Freight Train as we wound our way through the hills that day.

A FEW DAYS LATER, I flew a photographer into Iditarod late in the afternoon before the first mushers arrived. We slept in the mushers' tent, the temperature at 17 below, while we waited to see who would take on the "halfway jinx" and win the silver. No one in the history of the race had arrived first at the halfway point, taking the silver prize, and then gone on to win the gold at the finish line in Nome.

The next day, Jeff King was the first to round the bend and come into view of the waiting cameras. Not only did he accept the Iditadog Cafe for the joke it was, he is rumored to have paid for his hot dogs with a couple of the silver coins he won for getting there first.

I was given the job of hauling the rest of Jeff's 50 pounds of silver coins and the huge silver cup back to McGrath after ABC televised the halfway ceremony. Burt Bomhoff, then the executive director of the Iditarod Trail Committee, accompanied me. It was the same area that Freight Train and I had passed over a few days before. On the trip out, Burt and I saw caribou tracks on the low side-hills of nearly all the mountains before we spotted the one track we had hoped to see. A lone wolf track stretched out below us and disappeared on the treeless hillside horizons ahead. We decided to follow the track.

Before I knew it, I hadn't the foggiest notion where we were. I'll never understand how two mountain ridges got between us and where I thought we were. The skill of the early prospectors in finding their way around this area, let alone living and prospering here, is beyond me. Where the wolf trotted off to, only the caribou know. We never did find it. What I do know is that I'm thankful that the belly tank under my Cub had plenty of spare fuel when we started out that afternoon and that the runway lights at McGrath were operating when we arrived.

Less than a week after arriving at the Iditadog Cafe, Jeff King crossed under the arch in Nome to win the $50,000 first prize and become the first to break the halfway jinx.

26   All in *Good* Fun

If there is a group of volunteers along the trail that is even more close-knit than the pilots, it would have to be the trail breakers. And like the pilots, who start flying long before the gun goes off to start the race, the trail breakers are out the chute on the long haul to Nome before any dog hits the trail. Both groups enjoy a camaraderie that endures year-round.

Riding powerful snowmachines capable of getting to the finish line in a few days, these guys have to hold back and stay in front of the leading teams. It is not enough to mark the way to Nome; they now must "pave" the way. The trail breakers crawl up the trail, enduring the roughest of conditions for the sake of someone else's glory.

The trail breakers are the ones who mark out the dangerous ice crossings, cut logs to repair bridges, chop chunks of ice out of the way on the hundreds of streams that must be crossed. They are the ones who go into avalanche-prone areas, gingerly putting lath marking stakes over recent slides while craning their necks skyward, hoping the most recent snowfall stays put.

Like dog teams, snowmachines can be most uncooperative at times, especially when they are asked to plow uphill through man-size drifts of sugary snow. Breakdowns do occur, usually in the most awkward of places. Perhaps the snowmachine's greatest virtue compared with a dog team is that it won't run off even when it's not tethered to a tree.

When a snowmachine part or some other item is needed on the ground, the air force is only too happy to oblige. Air mail has a special meaning along the trail. For a trail breaker, usually the first indication of an incoming delivery is the roar of the airplane. Any good pilot can set up an approach without anyone on the ground seeing the plane. Suddenly roaring in low above a snowmachine is guaranteed to get the trail breaker's attention, alerting him to the package that is being tossed out of the plane. If the trail breaker thinks he has to duck or leap from his machine into the snow during this process, so much the better.

THE TRAIL BREAKERS AND THE PILOTS are good friends off the trail as well as when the race is in full swing. On the night after the first musher crosses the finish line in Nome, you can always count on the snowmachiners and the pilots to send a highly motivated delegation to that special event known as the Wet T-shirt Contest. It's not an official Iditarod event, but somehow this frontier-town contest has attracted a loyal following.

It's all in good fun, even if things tend to get a bit rowdy. When the town mayor vies for the job of master of ceremonies, you begin to see what long winters can do to folks in the far north. Put seven or eight hundred dollars in prize money on the event, and you attract not only some women who tend to be a bit exhibitionist in nature but also professional table-top dancers from the lustiest nighttime establishments of Anchorage or even the Lower 48.

How a stewardess from one of the Mark Air flights that landed at Nome that day got talked into entering the contest at the last moment by an Iditarod Air Force pilot leaves many questions unanswered. In any case, a costume was hurriedly assembled around her quite adequate features. What she lacked in professionalism, she more than made up for in beauty and innocence. Fortified at the last moment by two shots of Canadian Club, she timidly stepped up onto the stage. The front row went wild. A T-shirt and a pair of boxer shorts does little to cover up true innocence or a beauty that would have shown through even a flannel nightgown.

You bid and pay big bucks to be a wielder of one of the water squirt bottles. It wasn't long before every contestant was dripping wet from head to foot. Cleverly cut T-shirts disguised little.

Winners are selected by hand-clapping and cheering. The audience soon had it narrowed down to three finalists: a beautiful Native girl, a professional, and the boxer-clad flight attendant. In the front row, the trail breakers and the pilots outdid themselves in support of their favorite. Miss Boxer Shorts won the $800.

27 The Longest Night

Volunteer pilot George Murphy flew his Aeronca Sedan into the checkpoint at White Mountain one early afternoon to pick up a couple of passengers. He planned to fly race judge Jim Kershner and a veterinarian technician to Nome, only 60 air miles or so to the west. The weather was expected to deteriorate, but all that had materialized so far was a little wind.

George had flown in lots of wind over the years. As the second owner of the Aeronca that had come off the assembly line in 1948, George had worked it for the past twenty years all over the state. A project engineer, he had supervised the building of small airports and roads in just about every backwater community you could mention, and the Aeronca knew the way to and from each one.

At White Mountain, the technician had some tests to finish up. George decided to run Jim Kershner to Nome and then return for the technician, who had a commercial flight to catch out of Nome later that day. When they arrived in Nome, the wind was picking up, gusting to 30. Kershner thought George should forget about going back.

"It isn't worth busting up an airplane just so someone can make a flight," he told George.

But the technician wasn't the only person waiting for George in White Mountain. Dorothea—his constant companion, co-pilot, and wife—was also ready to fly out. George decided to return.

The wind wasn't so bad back at White Mountain, and George and the two women were soon airborne. But at Topkok, only about 15 miles away, troublesome winds were funneling down out of the mountains and onto Norton Sound.

During the current race, the concentrated winds at Topkok had forced more than one musher to take refuge in the shelter cabin. Topkok would be a bad place for an emergency landing, with wind-chill temperatures dropping at times below minus-100.

The wind was blowing 40 miles an hour, thrashing the Aeronca pretty hard. Pieces of survival gear that were stashed in the back were knocked forward more than once. Visibility was becoming poor. Nearing Solomon, George realized they were in trouble. He couldn't see anything up ahead, and turning back seemed risky. A turn to the left would put them over the water that had opened up during the day as ice moved away from the shoreline. To his right, inland, he saw only solid white, and he wanted none of that either.

Then he spotted the smooth ice of a small pond, a possible landing site. It was a gamble, but he didn't have to think about it for more than half a second. He pushed the Aeronca down onto the pond.

As the plane came to a halt on the ice, the wind was screaming. George knew he had to get ice screws down into the surface of the pond immediately so he would have something to tie the plane to. He gave the controls to Dorothea, so she could hold forward pressure on the yoke to keep the tail light and the airplane pointed into the wind.

Ice screws are mandatory equipment aboard all Iditarod Air Force planes. They are an expensive item at $30 or more each, but once you have used them, you don't ever go out in winter without at least three of them in your winter gear. These ingenious little devices, originally designed for use by mountain climbers, are nothing more than hollow tubes 7 or 8 inches long, with machined threads on the outside. Screwed into the ice, they will hold most anything—including a falling climber, or a grounded airplane being battered by high wind.

The technician, seated in back, had to step out into the wind so George could get in and find the ice screws stored under the back seat. He started handing items out to her to make room for his search—and her sleeping bag slipped loose, hurtling away into the swirling snow and toward the open water behind the plane. There was no time to chase it.

Then another setback: the centers of the ice screws were filled with ice and therefore couldn't be screwed in. (George had been forced to chop the screws out of the ice at Unalakleet, and they were still frozen solid.) With the head of an ax, he drove the screws at an angle into the ice as far as they would go and attached the tie-down ropes from the plane. It wasn't the best setup, but it was all he could do. They climbed back inside the plane, where the once-warm cabin had cooled to match the bone-numbing outside air. But at least they were out of the wind, which was now gusting to 50. There was nothing to do but wait and try to get warm.

Thanks to Dorothea, there was a good supply of munchies on board to stave off hunger. However, nothing could stop the cold that was driving in on them or the fine, dust-like snow that filtered through every crack. With one sleeping bag gone, they had to huddle together, with only two bags between the three of them.

The wind-driven tugging of the airplane against its tie-down ropes was interspersed with periods of sudden calm. At one point, George went outside to check the tie-downs, the only thing keeping them from being blown into Norton Sound. It was a dangerous move because the wind was blowing even harder. What little warmth the three of them had generated inside went out the door with George.

After that, George stayed inside, shining a flashlight out the Plexiglas windows many times to check the tie-downs. He was glad he had left some slack in the tail rope, for it relieved pressure on the wings each time the tail lifted off the ground. The roar of the wind was deafening. Sleep came in fits and starts.

Everyone heard the change in the wind—but even if they had been deaf, no one would have missed the terrifying feeling of the airplane being lifted off the ground. The

Aeronca hovered in the air for long moments. Blackness everywhere, open water somewhere behind them, and they were hanging on by threads that had been twisted and braided into rope that was tied to ice screws that couldn't be secured properly.

If the ropes snapped or the ice screws pulled free, the three people inside the plane would jump out into the blackness and the freezing cold. This was the contingency plan they had all discussed. No one was about to stay in an airplane that was sure to be blown into the water. George reckoned that the wind was now pushing 80 miles an hour.

In Nome, Jim Kershner and many others worried about the missing plane and its three occupants all through the long night. White Mountain had reported them leaving as scheduled, but no one had seen or heard from them since. There was nothing to do but wait until daylight would permit a search.

The winds had also battered Nome during the night. Dave Alborn, one of the few pilots able to get his plane up and running that morning, volunteered to go immediately in search of George.

The Aeronca's red wings and yellow body stood out like a beacon to Dave and the partner who accompanied him on the search. They were happy to find the plane, but it was the sight of the waving arms of three people that prompted the rescuers' wide grins. The long worry was over.

28 Ticket to Hell

Contrary to popular belief, a brand new instrument rating does not guarantee safer flights for a pilot. More than likely, the new ticket will sooner or later get that pilot into far more trouble than he or she would have had without one. With official recognition of your ability to fly on instruments alone when there's no visibility, you're ready to take chances you never would before. Sort of like the pilot who believes he can do anything just because he is flying a Super Cub. With an instrument ticket, you can go anywhere anytime. At least that's what the flight schools claim. It's an easy belief to fall into during good weather. But create a scenario with rotten weather, an apparent emergency, and a soft-hearted pilot with an instrument rating, and you've set the stage for disaster.

DANNY DAVIDSON, proud holder of the instrument ticket, was in McGrath when word came in about the injured musher. The emergency medical technician who tended to her had reported that she would lose a leg to amputation if she wasn't evacuated immediately from McGrath to Anchorage. The weather was poor in McGrath, and much worse toward the mountains. Ferocious winds were lashing McGrath, and the locals knew from long experience that the mountains nearer to Anchorage would be hit even harder. Night was close at hand.

Without the new license, Danny would have had to turn a deaf ear to the call for help. But soft-hearted as always—and with a brand new and unused instrument ticket burning a hole deep into his young pilot ego—he chose to disregard the deteriorating weather. He took the injured woman aboard his wheel-ski Cessna 180.

After getting FAA clearance, Danny taxied out past the last of the blue lights and onto the McGrath runway, where long rows of white lights pointed his airplane toward Anchorage. Darkness was swallowing the distant mountains as the 180 roared down the runway. Soon the worried onlookers heard only the sound of the wind as the plane disappeared into the evening sky. Danny could feel the wind buffeting the plane as they neared the mountains, but it wasn't bad. (It never is when there's still time to turn around.)

Over the mountains, it was a different story. The snow started falling in force, the gauges on his instruments were bouncing violently, and any turns were out of the question. In the fierce wind, Danny wasn't even sure the wings would stay on. His injured passenger was in the back seat, comfortably padded with cushions and cloth wing covers.

Danny was glad she wasn't up front with him to see how black black can be when you are surrounded with white.

Soon after the Anchorage flight center cleared him to descend, ice started to form on the windshield and wings. Danny was suddenly enrolled in a graduate course in instrument flying, learning things on the spot that they never taught him in school. Runway lights never looked better as he brought the 180 back to earth. But learning to land the plane safely under terrible conditions was only part of the education he would receive from this flight.

Danny was in Anchorage most of the next day before making contact with some pilot buddies at McGrath to verify the weather on that side of the mountains. What he learned has never left him. The musher he had delivered to a waiting ambulance the night before was already back in McGrath, hitching up her dogs to continue the race. She had taken a commercial flight back from Anchorage that morning. The only thing wrong with her leg was a slight sprain. Scenes from the grueling trip flashed before his eyes: the violence of the wind; the ice on the windshield; the fears that he would never see another day. He had risked everything for nothing.

YEARS LATER DANNY AGAIN risked it all on an instrument flight, but this time he wasn't asked to fly into the bad weather. The weather found him. Climbing to nearly a thousand feet as he left the Yukon River village of Grayling, en route to McGrath, Danny was unaware of anything out of the ordinary until suddenly everything went white. The snowstorm had come from behind. By now, the transition to instruments came easy. He headed higher and got on the radio.

"Hey Daryl, you got snow up there?"

Daryl Gareau, who lived in Grayling, had departed only minutes before Danny. He, too, was on his way to McGrath.

"No, it's fine here. Why?"

"I just went zero, zero. I can't be more than five or ten minutes behind you."

"How high are you?"

"I'm just coming up on twenty-four hundred feet now but I'm still climbing." Danny's voice showed little concern.

"You should pop out of it pretty soon." Daryl was casual as well, but he wondered about Danny in the snow behind him. It didn't make any sense. You always see it coming.

They were only minutes into the one-hour flight when Danny first called. Daryl waited until he saw the long-range radar site at Tatalina on Takotna Mountain, about 15 miles out of McGrath, before he checked back with Danny.

"How are you doing now, Dan?"

"Over eight thousand feet and still in it. I'm thinking I should head back towards Grayling and see if maybe it's blown through. How is it there?"

"I just took a look around and it's white everywhere back your way. Looks like I'm going to just beat it to McGrath. Why don't you make contact with the radar guys at Tatalina? Just in case."

"I'm going to turn around and see what's going on back on the river first. Should be able to see something pretty soon. Thanks. I'll call them then if I need to."

"The river's wide there and good to land on just about anywhere north of the village," Daryl said, referring to the Yukon above Grayling. "If you can make out the trees on either side, you should be able to put it down easily. Good luck."

"Thanks." Danny was on his own.

Flying back to where he began, he was still engulfed in snow. He didn't dare come below the minimum en-route altitude in order to look around. It was time to ask for help.

The Tatalina radar site came right back to him on the radio, but the report wasn't good. Snow now covered McGrath as well.

"Do you have enough fuel to get up to Galena, where you can shoot an instrument approach?" he was asked.

"No, I don't think so," Danny answered.

His voice no longer sounded as casual as when he was talking to Daryl.

The white that had filled his world since he left Grayling was now turning to gray as the unseen sun slipped lower in the west. Tatalina had a firm radar fix on Danny's 180. The crew there put him in line with the straight stretch of the Yukon near Grayling and gave guidance to ease him down through the ever-darkening snow soup.

An instrument approach to a known and lighted runway is bad enough. But he was coming down onto the untracked snow of a remote section of river, nearly in the dark and swallowed in swirling snow. The Cessna bounced before he realized he was on the ground. He was down and safe once again.

Prepared to spend a long night inside the cabin of the plane, Danny was dozing when a knock came on the door. It was someone on a snowmachine. Daryl had called to tell his wife of Danny's plight, and she had folks standing by the river, waiting. At the sound of Danny's plane, a couple of snowmachiners took off upriver to find him.

Thanks to his instrument skills, Danny was alive. And thanks to Daryl, Danny would soon be very comfortable, snuggled deep inside his sleeping bag by a cozy wood-fired barrel stove in the town hall.

29 Going Home

After weeks of flying the trail, an Iditarod pilot is ready for home sweet home. The end of the race usually finds a gang of pilots in Nome just itching to head south. And the itch only gets worse if they are weathered in or if the last of the mushers is slow in crossing the finish line.

It was the usual scenario in 1993. The race was over, the pilots and most everyone else were done with the work and the play, and home beckoned. Among the folks trying to get out of Nome that year was Chris O'Gar, a former musher who lives in McGrath. She served as a checker in McGrath, then managed to get herself smuggled up to the celebrations in Nome aboard an Iditarod Air Force plane.

Naturally all the homeward-bound pilots were more than ready to offer a ride back to McGrath to this cute little checker. The race manager was being stubborn, however. Chris was in Nome unofficially, so he refused to let her fly with any of the volunteer pilots. If any pilot took her aboard, the official warned, he would be dropped from the list of insured pilots. Sometimes the thinking of the powers-that-be leaves much to be desired. All the volunteers should have the chance to get to Nome at least once.

At this point, George Murphy came to the rescue. George, who was pushing sixty-five, had been part of the Iditarod Air Force for as long as anyone could remember. A congenial fellow, he is one of those guys you can't help but like. In 1992, George handled the nearly thankless job of chief pilot and, like Larry Thompson, finally drifted away from involvement with the air force to take on some commercial work during the race.

Officially, George has nothing to do with the Iditarod Air Force while he is carrying paying passengers. However, before and after the race and whenever he can squeeze it in, George lends a helping hand. So when he learned of Chris O'Gar's plight, he didn't hesitate to offer a ride in his Aeronca Sedan so that she could get back to McGrath without having to cough up the commercial fare.

When you think about it, George was probably the perfect person to handle the job of flying a good-looking woman from one place to another. He's had a lot of practice at it. Nome's KNOM radio station had assigned two young, vivacious female reporters to follow the mushers the entire length of the race, and George had been hired to haul them along the trail.

If you didn't know George, you might think he was tongue-tied in the presence of such charming company. But it was merely that George stuttered, so sometimes his words were slow in coming. Iditarod pilots still get a chuckle out of recalling the day George kept a group of planes stacked up in the air over Galena while he communicated with the control tower.

The Galena airport is manned by personnel of that other air force, the one run by the U.S. government. In marginal weather, several planes of the Iditarod Air Force were trying to get clearance from the U.S. Air Force people to land at Galena at about the same time. It was George who made the first contact with the tower.

The air controller had no way of knowing, when she asked George to give her a report on the weather, that it would take so long. The other pilots had little choice but to sweat it out while George struggled through his message. The weather was deteriorating rapidly. All that the pilots wanted was to receive landing clearance and get safely on the ground. That's all George wanted, too. Eventually they all got what they wanted, but it took a while.

THE WEATHER WAS GLORIOUS on the day that George flew on his way to McGrath with Chris as his passenger. The rest of the guys also loaded up their planes and departed at the same time as George for the long haul toward home. All the checkpoints back down the trail beyond Unalakleet had been cleaned up. Most of the pilots were heading for the Anchorage area, and a fuel stop in McGrath was all that was in the way between Nome and home. It had been a long race when you realize that some of the fellows had started hauling pre-race loads in mid-February. April would be upon them in less than a week.

After a stop in McGrath to let Chris off and to refuel, the planes were on their way again. The relief of going home was apparent in everyone's voice, even over the radio. Now that the storms and the cold and the strain of ten long post-race days in Nome were over, no one seemed to have a care in the world. As they flew toward Rainy Pass and Anchorage, there was no lack of radio chatter.

It is no wonder the Iditarod Trail Committee finally put some limits on how long a dog team can stay on the trail after the main body of racers reaches Nome. It's easy to forget that as long as a musher is still on the trail, the work of the volunteers is not done. Volunteers staff all the checkpoints. They care for all the dogs that are dropped off and handle the thousand and two logistical items that need attention. There is at least one volunteer for each dog that heads up the trail, and the volunteer organization is as much a wonder as the race itself.

While the pilots are only a small fraction of the entire group of Iditarod helpers, it's doubtful that many volunteers stay with the race longer than those who fly the trail in the airplanes they own (and "donate" with some regularity to the cause). You really have to love flying to volunteer yourself and your airplane for the Iditarod. Although airplane insurance has finally become part of the package, it can never cover the anguish of losing what to some is their most prized possession.

It would be hard to calculate the financial losses these volunteers have endured since the time Larry Thompson cartwheeled his Cessna 180 in the early days of the Iditarod. Jim Kershner, who has worn every conceivable badge identified with the Iditarod (except that of veterinarian), thinks that on average, an airplane a year has been lost since the race began in 1973. Common sense says it would be cheaper, if you thought you were going to lose your bird, to just send the Iditarod a check for $50,000 and let the airplane sit at home. Common sense also says that heading south in March would be wiser than heading into the mountains and up the trail to the arctic coast, where weather and misfortune are always waiting for the unwary.

But flying is a high, literally. There is nothing that cures the flying bug except more flying. And if the flying can be done in some of the most beautiful surroundings in the world, so much the better. For this special group of pilots, the race above the trail each March is something they need as much as a dog team needs a place to run.

The volunteer pilots are prepared to risk their all for the chance to do the flying they love. But when these guys have had their fun, they are ready for the most important thing of all, going home. For George and the other pilots flying toward Anchorage, the race was over for another year. As the planes drew nearer to home, someone finally asked George the question everyone wanted an answer to.

"George? You on?"

"Yu . . . yu . . . yeh . . . yes!"

"How is it you always seem to end up with the cute chicks?"

Long pause.

"Hmmm . . . ahhh . . . it . . . it . . . it's the airplane!"

Ted Mattson with his Super Cub *Baldy Bluebird.*

About the Author

Ted Mattson, born in Pennsylvania in 1939, earned a degree in agronomy from Penn State. After a tour in the Army, during which he received pilot training, he pursued his original career in turf grass management, specializing in golf courses. He and his wife, Penny, raised a daughter, Maria. The lure of Alaska brought him north, where he flew a helicopter on the North Slope. He later joined the salmon fishery in Bristol Bay. With his divorce in 1982, Alaska became his permanent home.

An avid outdoorsman, Ted volunteered as a pilot with the Iditarod Air Force for four years. He has worked as a big-game guide, flown helicopters from tuna boats in the South Pacific, and dived on the Great Barrier Reef in Australia. He dabbles in gold prospecting, hunts with a bow and arrow, sportfishes with a fly rod, and loves wood-and-canvas canoes.

Ted recently gave up his Piper Super Cub *Baldy Bluebird* as down payment on *Skookumchuck,* a 53-foot, ketch-rigged motor-sailer, which he uses in Southeast Alaska for halibut fishing and giving eco-tours. He also continues gillnetting for salmon in Bristol Bay. He is author of *The Eye of the Rainbow,* which chronicles his adventures as he pursued his dream of living in Alaska.

FLYING COLD

THE ADVENTURES OF RUSSEL MERRILL, PIONEER ALASKAN AVIATOR

By Robert Merrill MacLean and Sean Rossiter

Trained as a pilot during World War I, Russel Merrill was determined to spend his life flying. His love of flight lured him to Alaska, where Merrill piloted the first airplanes to fly into Petersburg, Wrangell, Kodiak, and Anchorage. He challenged dangerous terrain, severe climates, and mechanical failures to bring aviation to remote communities. Merrill forever changed northern history and commerce as a prominent member of the territory's first graduating class of bush pilots who earned their wings in the school of hard-earned experience.

"A good well-illustrated book does what a good movie does . . . all at once you're there with Russ Merrill standing alongside his old Travel Air on one of Anchorage's bitter winter days. You stare at the open cockpit and feel the bite of the wind and it comes to you what kind of man this was and how really tough he was challenging, even unsuccessfully, the savage skies of the North."

—*General Aviation News & Flyer*

192 pages; 10" by 9"; 75 black and white photos.
ISBN: 0-945397-32-1 (HB); 0-945397-33-X (PB)

For a copy of *Flying Cold,* visit your local bookstore. Or send a check for $34.95 hardbound or $24.95 paperback (plus 8.2% tax on orders from Washington state) and $3 postage/handling to: Epicenter Press, Box 82368, Kenmore, WA 98028. Visa/MC: phone 206-485-6822 or fax 206-481-8253.